W9-DJO-135

Law and State

THE CASE OF NORTHERN IRELAND

KEVIN BOYLE, TOM HADDEN,
PADDY HILLYARD

Martin Robertson · London

University of Massachusetts Press · Amherst

First published 1975 in Great Britain by Martin Robertson and
Company, 17 Quick Street, London N1 8HL, and published in
the United States of America by the University of Massachusetts
Press, Amherst, Massachusetts.

Library of Congress Catalog Card Number 75–10914

ISBN 0–87023–197–9

Law and State was originally published in Great Britain in a series
entitled *Law in Society* edited by C. M. Campbell, W. G. Carson
and P. N. P. Wiles

Set by Trade Linotype Ltd., Birmingham
Printed and bound in Great Britain by
Redwood Burn Limited, Trowbridge & Esher

CONTENTS

INTRODUCTORY NOTE

The troubles in Northern Ireland over the past six years have been and continue to be one of the most inflammatory issues in contemporary British politics. Yet for all that the majority of the citizens of the United Kingdom remain ignorant of the nature and dimensions of the problem. Northern Ireland has been bracketed off: the geographical divide of the Irish Sea has apparently allowed the turmoil in the province to be isolated as part of a separate political reality. Northern Ireland has been defined as just another troubled, distant place; in the rest of the United Kingdom this is manifested in emotional outcry or in a crude neo-colonialist attitude to the 'Irish problem'. The administration of law in Northern Ireland, for example, has been changed in ways which, had they occurred in the rest of the Kingdom, would have been perceived as radically altering the nature of the 'legal order'. But as a consequence of the distancing of Northern Ireland these changes have not been seen as necessitating a reappraisal of the nature and operation of law in the rest of the country.

In the United Kingdom there are differing substantive laws, court structures and legal procedures in the different jurisdictions of England, Scotland and Northern Ireland. In spite of this it has been traditionally espoused that there is a shared adherence to 'the rule of law', with a similar notion of legal order prevailing; thus the variations have been presented as matters of detail and of secondary importance. Yet the administration of law in Northern Ireland, and the changes in procedures adopted in the province in recent years, can only be understood if a rather different concept of legal order is first adopted. This leads to a fundamental questioning of the rule of law in Great Britain.

vii

Such questions have not been raised because Northern Ireland has been treated as a separate problem – though the very separation argues against the acceptance of the rule of law in the United Kingdom.

For the academic a sociology of law must inquire into the nature of legal legitimacy: to what extent and in what ways is the law as a specific institution able to contribute to social order? To embark on such inquiry in times of political and social stability is rendered difficult by the fact that the sociological enterprise itself takes place within the order so created. Things which may be problematic are taken for granted precisely because they are tacit elements of that order. To overcome this involves transcending the nature of the current social order, and it is this that makes the sociology of law such a difficult undertaking. Yet when the legality of law is attacked, when the basis of legitimacy is challenged, when there is a constitutional crisis, and obligation to the law is denied, aspects of the legal order which are previously concealed become visible, the problematic nature of legal legitimacy is starkly revealed. In such times the need for study of the character of the law, its relationship to the state, its reaction to such pressure, is greater. Official reports appear but the very nature of the challenge to the state renders them problematic elements in the situation; the authority which normally attaches to such reports is exactly what is being questioned. Apart from official reports however there have been very few attempts to assess the implications of legal change in Northern Ireland and that alone makes the present monograph an important document for the political debate in Britain.

The authors examine critically the nature and operation of law in Northern Ireland and underscore the response of the law to the troubled history of the province. Yet Northern Ireland is not an isolated or separate entity and the fundamental questions that are raised for the whole legal order in the United Kingdom are highlighted. The relevance of the study to contemporary political debate is obvious in that it will allow all citizens of the United Kingdom to examine what has been done in their name, and in the name of law, in one part of the United Kingdom. It is also part of the continuing attempt to understand and explain order and law, and as such it has implications far beyond its immediate context.

C.M.C.
W.G.C.
P.N.P.W.

1. INTRODUCTION

It is a commonplace of sociology that the functioning of a state and its legal system are closely intertwined. In settled times this fact may become obscured. The apparent independence of the legal system from current political disputes lends support to the myth that law is something above and apart from the society which it helps to regulate and control. An alternative view is that law is nothing but an instrument of domination in the hands of the property owners or the political elite. This is equally unsatisfactory. Adherence to either view serves only to obscure the kernel of truth which lies behind them both, that a legal system may reflect both the values and the power structure of the state.

The key to the paradox lies in the fact that these relationships are not static. In times of stability the prevailing value system is the determining factor and the power structure remains very much in the background. In times of political and social disruption value systems recede into the background and the reality of political, economic and military power is likely to prevail.

This pattern can be simply illustrated.

In a settled state the most obvious function of the legal system is the resolution of individual disputes within the existing value system. But the law also plays a part in maintaining the political and social stability which allows the whole system to operate smoothly.

In a democratic system of government that stability is dependent on the existence of adequate channels for the resolution of deeply felt grievances. The primary channel for this purpose is political. Ideally grievances are raised on behalf of those concerned or affected by their parliamentary representatives, who will seek to have things put right by direct political

1

pressure on the government. In practice pressure of this kind can now often be marshalled with equal or greater force through radio and television, but the principle is the same. The effectiveness of the campaign is determined in either case by a mixture of the merits of the case, the strength of public opinion on the issue and the government's own political commitments. There is no right to redress in politics; but in an open democratic system there is a fair chance of securing some measure of satisfaction.

It is when political pressures prove insufficient that the second channel of redress through legal action becomes important. This is more limited. It applies only in respect of certain more fundamental grievances, and in particular the abuse of governmental power. Under the common law and under most written constitutions there is a formal right, which can be pursued in the courts, to remedy any unlawful, arbitrary or biased exercise of power or force contrary to the rule of law.

Public confidence in the existence and efficacy of these two channels of redress is essential to the smooth working of democracy. Where it is absent the temptation to resort to violence and terrorism to draw attention to deeply felt grievances may be very strong. Under some circumstances direct action of this kind may prove highly effective, if only in creating a sense of urgency in ordinary political channels. But where there are opposing factions, each of which is prepared to resort to such tactics or is liable to express its feelings in that way, there is an obvious risk that violence from one faction will merely prove a stimulus to a violent response from the other faction, and that there will be a progressive escalation in group conflict towards anarchy and civil war. This risk is particularly great where, as in Ireland, there is a lively tradition of paramilitary activity.

When violence of this kind does break out the legal system is faced with an equally fundamental function, that of dealing with civil disorder and terrorism. Its effectiveness in so doing is also dependent on the extent of public confidence in the justice both of individual trials and of any emergency measures which are taken. Decisions or measures which are seen by any substantial section of the population as unjust are likely to lead to an increase rather than a decrease in disorder and violence. Yet the legal system by its very constitution is committed to the protection of the existing state. Where the conflict is of a revolutionary kind it is almost inevitable that the legal system will be seen as supporting one or other faction in the conflict. And to that extent the maintenance of general public confidence in its operation may become increasingly difficult. The confidence of the dominant faction will be eroded by decisions and measures which appear to condone disorder and violence directed against the state, while that of the opposing faction will be eroded by decisions or measures which appear to derogate from accepted standards of legality.

The problems faced by a legal system in this context are not eased by the fact that public confidence is not necessarily an accurate reflection of the true state of affairs. Lack of confidence in a judicial system may be a result of irrational perceptions. Satisfactory channels for the redress of grievances may not be properly tested as a result of a prior lack of confidence in the prospects of success. Perfectly just or justifiable decisions or measures may be perceived as unjust on the basis of highly selective comparisons. Lack of confidence is a social phenomenon which may spring from relatively small causes and feed on itself.

A further complicating factor which may interfere with these relatively simple political and social processes is the internal structure of the legal system. The law itself enshrines certain basic values and procedures which are not easily altered. The legal profession, the police and the army are likewise institutions with a built-in commitment to certain values and methods of operating which are highly resistant to rapid or radical change, whether by statutory or administrative reform.

The case of Northern Ireland is a particularly striking example of all these features of the relationships between law and state in both relatively peaceful and highly disturbed conditions. It demonstrates very clearly the basic connection between the legal system and the state which it helps to support, and the related fact that when that state is threatened the legal system will be used on behalf of the state by those in power in whatever way seems to them most likely to restore stability. It shows the practical importance of public confidence in the legal system if stability is to be regained without relying solely on superior force. And it underlines the constraints which are imposed on the

3

government by the internal structures and values of the legal system and the agencies of law and order.

The framework for this analysis is the story of the operation of the legal system in Northern Ireland from the start of the civil rights movements in the mid-1960s to a situation which some were describing as incipient civil war at the end of 1974. Telling this story presents certain problems of organisation. Ideally every legal event would be considered in the light of the current political situation. But an attempt to explain to those not already acquainted with the intricacies of Ulster politics the full story of the past decade is far beyond the scope of this book. Instead we have sought to give a general introduction to the Northern Ireland problem in the context of an account of the legal response to the initial phase of relatively peaceful civil rights agitation. This is followed by a brief summary of the development of terrorism and of military and sectarian violence from 1969 onwards, to set in context the more detailed analysis of the operation of various aspects of the legal system under emergency conditions in the chapters which follow. These deal in turn with the system for the arrest and interrogation of suspected terrorists, the system of internment without trial and finally the operation of the ordinary courts in those cases in which formal criminal proceedings were brought. We have then sought to give a picture of ordinary people's attitudes to the legal system as a whole, drawing both on the published statements of various pressure groups and commentators and on a small survey of public attitudes carried out in the summer of 1974. Finally we have sought to put the resulting picture of the operation of the legal system in Northern Ireland in times of acute internal disorder in its historical context by looking briefly at similar issues as they have emerged in the continuing troubled relationship between Britain and Ireland in the past two or three hundred years. This historical dimension may help to add some further weight to our general conclusions on the subject of law and state in the concluding chapter.

Much of the material on which this book is based was collected primarily with a view to influencing the course of events. Much of it has already been published or submitted to various governmental bodies.[1] To that extent we do not claim to be wholly objective observers, even if that were possible for anyone living in such a complex and emotionally charged situation as that now prevailing in Northern Ireland. But we have sought in this presentation to focus attention on those factors which transcend the particular situations to which we directed our research and recommendations.

NOTES AND REFERENCES

1. Much of the material relating to the period up to 1973 is taken from *Justice in Northern Ireland – A Study in Social Confidence* by Tom Hadden and Paddy Hillyard, published by the Cobden Trust in October 1973; much of the material relating to the subsequent period is taken from a submission by the authors to the Gardiner Committee set up in June 1974 to consider the operation of the Northern Ireland (Emergency Provisions) Act 1973.

2. CIVIL RIGHTS:
THE FAILURE OF LAW AND OF LAYWERS

The state of Northern Ireland was created in 1921 as a by-product of the failure of the last of a long series of British proposals for the conferment of a limited degree of autonomy on Ireland as a whole. The Northern Protestants had armed themselves to resist 'home rule' as early as 1912. When in 1920 and 1921 the predominantly Roman Catholic population of the southern counties of Ireland took up arms against the British and eventually gained their independence as the Irish Free State (later the Republic of Ireland), the Northern Protestants under the leadership of the Unionist Party opted for a measure of local autonomy within the United Kingdom as provided in the Government of Ireland Act 1920. This statute originally envisaged the establishment of local parliaments both in the northern six counties and in the southern twenty-six counties, and also provided machinery which might lead to the eventual unity of the two parts of the country, but its effective operation was limited to the six counties of Northern Ireland. After a brief period of armed conflict in 1921 and 1922 the Unionists' para-military police forces, known as the Specials, with the assistance of the British Army established the authority of the new parliament and government in the six county area. This settlement was imposed by force of arms upon a reluctant Roman Catholic minority which formed approximately one third of the total population of Northern Ireland as a whole, and roughly one half of the population in the border counties of Fermanagh and Tyrone.

In theory Northern Ireland was established as a non-sectarian state in which the basic democratic rights of all citizens were constitutionally guaranteed. The Government of Ireland Act 1920 made specific provision to that effect, notably in declaring void any law enacted by the new parliament which gave preference, privilege or advantage or imposed disability or disadvantage on account of religious belief. The reality was otherwise. The proud promise of a 'Protestant parliament for a Protestant people' was effectively fulfilled through the continued stranglehold of the exclusively Protestant Unionist Party in the parliament at Stormont. The system of local government was also so organised as to guarantee the dominance of the Unionists even in areas where they were outnumbered. And the fundamental legal rights of all citizens against arbitrary arrest and imprisonment were effectively annulled by the provisions of the Civil Authorities (Special Powers) Act of 1922, which was re-enacted from year to year until 1933 when it was made permanent. The powers of arrest and detention under the Special Powers Act, as it was generally known, were not formally directed against Roman Catholics and Republicans, but it was common knowledge that it was against them and them alone that it was directed and used. On each occasion that Republican militants, whether from north or south of the border, resumed their active campaign for the reunification of Ireland by force, as in 1938 and 1956, substantial numbers of leading Republican politicians and activists were interned without trial. In this way the Unionists made use of the legal system to secure themselves both against peaceful political challenge and against internal and external terrorist attacks. They regarded themselves as being fully justified in so doing by the refusal of the government of the Republic of Ireland and of many Roman Catholics in Northern Ireland to recognise the legitimacy of their state, and by the periodic resumption of hostilities by the IRA.

Most members of the Roman Catholic minority in Northern Ireland, whose basic aspiration was and remains the unification of Northern Ireland with the Republic, regarded this use of the legal system to support the Unionist state as wholly unjustifiable. Militant Republicans refused to recognise the legitimacy of Northern Ireland courts, and many other Roman Catholics continued to distrust the whole legal system as the puppet of the Unionists. Consequently, though there is little doubt that some

7

Unionist practices were a direct or indirect infringement of the constitutional guarantees against discrimination in the Government of Ireland Act, no serious legal challenge to the Unionist regime was mounted prior to the civil rights campaign of 1968 and 1969. On a political level too the minority continued to regard the Unionist government as wholly unresponsive to any form of reasoned argument on matters which concerned the allocation of political power and patronage. In most areas the Roman Catholic community maintained its separate social and political identity, not least through its separate educational system, and practised the politics of abstention.

The Civil Rights Movement

The first signs of a change in this attitude became apparent in the early 1960s. A number of Roman Catholic politicians and leaders began to assert a series of claims for more equal treatment for Roman Catholics within the state of Northern Ireland. This civil rights campaign, as it came to be known in more or less direct imitation of the example of the Blacks in the United States, covered a whole range of economic and political grievances, but was centred on a number of fundamental democratic claims: the right to participate in the election of central and local government through a scupulously fair electoral system; the right to pursue legitimate political and social objectives without interference from government; the right to share equitably in the allocation of state resources; and the right to freedom from arbitrary arrest or detention. In the specific Northern Ireland context attention was focussed primarily on allegations of the gerrymandering of electoral boundaries, of discrimination in public housing and employment and in the implementation of government schemes for social welfare and economic development, and of the infringement of basic legal rights under the Special Powers Act.

It is now generally accepted that these allegations were well founded. The Cameron Commission on Disturbances in Northern Ireland, set up in August 1969 in the immediate aftermath of the

8

widespread rioting and disorder in Londonderry, Belfast and some other towns, concluded that the following items were major factors in the outbreak of the disturbances:

(1) A rising sense of continuing injustice and grievance among large sections of the Catholic population in Northern Ireland, in particular in Londonderry and Dungannon, in respect of (i) inadequacy of housing provision by certain local authorities (ii) unfair methods of allocation of houses built and let by such authorities, in particular refusals and omissions to adopt a 'points' system in determining priorities and making allocations (iii) misuse in certain cases of discretionary powers of allocation of houses in order to perpetuate Unionist control of the local authority.

(2) Complaints, now well documented in fact, of discrimination in the making of local government appointments, at all levels but especially in senior posts, to the prejudice of non-Unionists and especially Catholic members of the community, in some Unionist controlled authorities.

(3) Complaints, again well documented, in some cases of deliberate manipulation of local government electoral boundaries and in others a refusal to apply for their necessary extension, in order to achieve and maintain Unionist control of local authorities and so to deny to Catholics influence in local government proportionate to their numbers.[1]

To these might be added the specific complaint at the siting of most new economic development in the mainly Protestant area east of the River Bann, and in particular the foundation of the New University of Ulster at Coleraine rather than Londonderry. The Cameron Commission also referred to the resentment among the Roman Catholic community at the continued existence of the Special Powers Act and the exclusively Protestant 'B Specials', a paramilitary police force which had survived from the troubles of the 1920s, both of which were designed and used to protect the Unionist state from internal subversion or external attack by Republicans.

The Failure to Obtain a Legal Remedy

The Cameron Commission concentrated its attention on the frustration within the Roman Catholic community at the failure of political pressure to induce the governments at Westminster and Stormont to investigate and remedy these grievances. This was understandable, since it was through political channels that the civil rights campaign had been pursued. But the failure of the civil rights leaders to make any sustained attempt to obtain a legal remedy for their grievances also requires some explanation. It is a primary task of law and lawyers to deal with basic grievances of this kind before recourse is made to direct action, with all the risks of riot and disorder which that may bring in its train. Why was it that in Northern Ireland this essential safety valve of legal redress was not there to avert the confrontation which developed?

The most obvious explanation for this failure of law and lawyers was the absence of any formal guarantees in the British and Northern Irish constitution of basic civil rights and the consequent lack of any tradition of civil rights litigation. This is in direct contrast to the situation in the United States and in the Republic of Ireland where such formal guarantees are included in written constitutions and have been relied on in court actions. The part played by the United States Supreme Court in the development of civil rights is well known. Some militant Black leaders and white observers have admittedly laid emphasis on the dangerous effects of Supreme Court judgments in raising expectations which could not in the event be satisfied by purely legal means, but the US example has shown the value of fundamental legal and constitutional guarantees.

The difference in legal tradition, however, is not a sufficient explanation of the course of events in Northern Ireland. The absence of formal constitutional guarantees in the British constitution did not mean that abuses of the kind alleged in Northern Ireland could not have been remedied at law. The use of statutory powers in bad faith or for an improper purpose is an established ground of legal challenge in English law. It seems likely that this objection could have been raised in respect of the more blatant instances of electoral gerrymandering with a genuine prospect of success, at least in those areas where local wards were so drawn that a substantial majority of Catholics were continually outvoted in local elections by a minority of Unionists. Furthermore, the specific constitutional guarantees

10

against discriminatory legislation in the Government of Ireland Act could well have formed the basis of a challenge to the validity of discriminatory administrative decisions made under Northern Ireland statutes, for instance in the field of housing allocation, as well as to the statutes themselves. This possibility was clearly stated in the leading text book on constitutional law.[2]

Nor can the failure to pursue the civil rights campaign in the courts in preference to the streets be attributed to a lack of organisation or finance. At the party political level there was a lack of effective organisation and expertise among Nationalist and Republican representatives. There was no central party organisation or national conference until 1966. Candidates for elections were selected by ad hoc meetings of local notables, and after election pursued their own individual strategies and policies. But the Campaign for Social Justice, a highly professional and committed propaganda and action group centred in Dungannon, had been in existence since 1963 and from around 1966 there was a much greater degree of organisation and co-ordination among opposition MPs throughout Northern Ireland. There can be little doubt that these forces would have had little difficulty in raising the necessary funds and backing for a serious legal challenge to the various discriminatory practices maintained by local Unionist councils had they been convinced of the prospects of making any progress.

The necessary confidence in the judicial system as a means of securing justice, however, appears to have been lacking. It is difficult to produce firm evidence on matters of this kind other than the failure of civil rights leaders to initiate any legal action prior to the Republican Clubs case in 1968, and the Dungannon housing litigation in 1970/71. The attitude of the Campaign for Social Justice, which was perhaps the most likely sponsor of action in this field, is significant. The committee had assembled a sufficiently impressive dossier of discrimination in 1963 to make a direct approach to the British Prime Minister, Sir Alec Douglas-Home. Sir Alec responded by recommending legal action in the courts, though he also applied secret pressure on the Ulster Premier, Captain Terence O'Neill, to do something about the general situation. After this apparent failure on the political front the committee did approach counsel for an opinion on the

11

prospects of challenging the Dungannon Council on housing allocation, and received first a negative and then a guarded but reasonably favourable opinion, based on an assessment of the legal position by Harry Calvert of the Law Faculty of Queen's University, Belfast. But when their application for legal aid to pursue the action was turned down by the Legal Aid Committee, and on appeal, the matter was not pursued. The Campaign for Social Justice clearly regarded this rebuff as further evidence of the essential bias in the system, and reverted to the view that, after six or seven years of effort with local lawyers, none of whom appeared to have any fire in their bellies, there was no future in legal redress.[3]

The simplest explanation for the persistence of this attitude was the feeling in Republican circles that the courts and the judiciary were part and parcel of the Unionist power structure and therefore unlikely to uphold any serious challenge to the regime. It is incontrovertible that the majority of judicial appointments in Northern Ireland had been made from the ranks of Unionism. Of twenty High Court judges appointed since the independent Northern Ireland courts were established, fifteen had been openly associated with the Unionist Party: of twenty-three County Court appointments, fourteen had been visibly connected with the Unionist administration. At the height of the civil rights campaign in the late 1960s two of the three judges in the Northern Ireland Court of Appeal were ex-Attorney-Generals in Unionist governments; one of the four High Court judges was likewise an ex-Attorney-General, and another the son of an Attorney-General; two of the five County Court judges were ex-Unionist MPs and another the son of a Unionist MP; and among the twelve Resident Magistrates there was an ex-Unionist MP, an ex-Unionist Senator, a defeated Unionist candidate and a former legal adviser to the Ministry of Home Affairs.[4]

The significance of these political appointments can be over-emphasised. There was an established tradition in all the jurisdictions of the British Isles, which has only recently been discarded, of raising ex-Attorney-Generals to the bench. Similar political affiliations of the kind alleged against Northern Ireland judges and magistrates could thus be raised against many judges in Britain and the Republic of Ireland.[5] But in Northern Ireland the permanent control of the Unionist Party at all levels of government lent a special force to complaints about political appointments. High Court appointments were the responsibility of the Westminster government which clearly followed a policy of ensuring that at least one senior judicial appointment was held by a Roman Catholic. But this did not apply to County Court or Magistrates Court appointments. Nor was there an opportunity for 'the other side' to restore the balance in its period of office as in other jurisdictions. Those members of the minority community who were appointed to judicial office were in any event regarded as 'Castle Catholics', more likely than not to support the government which had promoted them.

It does not follow from the preponderance of 'Unionists' on the bench in Northern Ireland that a challenge to the Unionist administration at central or local government level would necessarily have failed. Adherence to the role of impartial judicial decision-making by 'political' appointees has sometimes led to remarkable changes in apparent political leanings.[6] Nonetheless it can hardly be doubted that the composition of the judiciary did have an adverse effect on the confidence of the minority in the prospects of mounting a successful civil rights challenge in the courts. And when a case was finally raised on the banning of Republican clubs under the Special Powers Act, this assessment was apparently fully borne out. Whether this decision is to be attributed to political bias or to legal doctrine is a matter of debate. The performance of the Northern Ireland High Court judges in subsequent civil rights cases, in which challenges to the executive were regularly upheld, would be sufficient to dispel a charge of any continuing political bias to any reasonably objective observer. But by then the spotlight of world attention had been focussed on Northern Ireland, the reality of complaints of gerrymandering and discrimination had been officially recognised and a programme of reforms initiated. The importance of the Republican Clubs affair as a test case on the practicability of pursuing the civil rights campaign through the courts cannot be overestimated.

The Republican Clubs Case

In March 1967, the Ministry of Home Affairs made a regulation under the Special Powers Act adding to the list of unlawful associations: 'the organisations at the date of this regulation or at any time thereafter describing themselves as "republican clubs" or any like organisation howsoever described'. The addition appears to have been made in response to the growing civil rights agitation in traditionally Republican circles as an indication that the government would stand no nonsense from that quarter. But no serious attempt was made to enforce the regulation either on its introduction or subsequently.[7] The only case arising from the ban was in the nature of a test case against a Mr McEldowney who was charged in March 1968 with being a member of the Slaughtneil Republican Club. It seems certain that the prosecution was initiated by the authorities in order to test the legality of the regulation. No similar action was taken against any other Republican club and this case was taken to the House of Lords. The local magistrates dismissed the charge on the ground that the club in question could not be held to be unlawful as constituting a threat to peace and order in Northern Ireland within the terms of the regulation as they interpreted it. The Northern Ireland Court of Appeal reversed this decision on the ground that it was for the Minister of Home Affairs alone to decide whether a particular organisation should be deemed to be unlawful. But the Lord Chief Justice of Northern Ireland, Lord MacDermott, gave a strong dissenting judgment on the ground that the regulation as a whole was far too vague and wide to be capable of being related to the purpose prescribed in the Special Powers Act as being necessary for preserving peace and maintaining order in Northern Ireland. It is noteworthy that though one of the majority judges was a 'political' appointment in the sense of having been a Unionist Attorney-General, the dissenting judge Lord MacDermott had been in exactly the same position.

The case came before the House of Lords in London in April 1969, and the appeal was dismissed by a majority of three law lords to two on 18th June. The majority held that in the absence of proof of bad faith, which was not alleged, it was for the Minister alone to decide on the subversive nature of any organ-

14

isation, and that in the circumstances the words 'or any like organisation howsoever described' were not too wide to be supported. Lord Justice Diplock and Lord Justice Pearce dissented on similar grounds to those argued by Lord MacDermott, that since the magistrates had found as a fact that the Slaughtneil Republican Club had no seditious pursuits, a finding based on evidence given by the local police, it could not be argued that Republican clubs as a class had unlawful objects; they further argued that the use of the words 'or any like organisation howsoever described' rendered the regulation so vague as to fall outside the powers delegated to the Minister by the Act.[8]

The decision of the House of Lords in this case was in line with the prevailing British approach to constitutional law in refusing to challenge ministerial discretion in the absence of clear proof of bad faith. But in the context of Northern Ireland it was the final proof to the minority community that they could expect no aid from Britain in their struggle for what they regarded as their legitimate civil rights. Whether there was any element of political bias in the majority judgment either in the Northern Ireland Court of Appeal or even in the House of Lords must remain a matter of opinion. But there can be no doubt of its symbolic importance in showing the futility of pursuing the civil rights campaign through the courts. It is significant that the forces of law and order in Derry and Belfast broke down within weeks of the final rejection of the claim in the House of Lords.

Subsequent Civil Rights Legislation: The Reform Programme

The violence of August 1969 and the arrival of British troops inevitably shifted the focus of attention away from internal civil rights litigation. Northern Ireland became a major political issue in the British Parliament and in the Republic of Ireland. The UK and Northern Ireland premiers met in London and issued a joint declaration confirming the constitutional position of Northern Ireland as part of the United Kingdom and thus the ultimate responsibility of the United Kingdom government, and affirming the right of its citizens, irrespective of political views or religion, to the same equality of treatment and freedom from discrimination in all legislation and executive decisions of government as obtained in the rest of the United Kingdom.[9] Agreement was also reached on the broad outlines of a reform programme based on these principles.

The basis of this programme was not the creation of legally enforceable rights but the setting up of new or reformed institutions and agencies. The structure of the police force and the special constabulary was to be reviewed by leading British police chiefs; the reform of local government, incorporating universal adult franchise and an independent commission responsible for electoral boundaries, was to be pressed through; and equality of opportunity in public employment and fairness in the allocation of public housing was to be guaranteed by the appointment of parliamentary and local government ombudsmen. It was also agreed that it was vital that the momentum of these internal reforms be maintained.

It may be that these measures would have been sufficient to meet the legitimate complaints of the Roman Catholic community, though there were some important omissions, notably on discrimination in private employment. But the pace and manner of implementation was certainly not sufficient to gain their confidence or meet their expectations. As 1969 and 1970 dragged on with little outward sign of any improvement on any of the main civil rights issues protest marches and rioting continued on a sporadic basis. Confrontations with troops and police became more and more frequent in the Roman Catholic enclaves of Belfast and Derry. There was a progressive escalation in the violence of the tactics employed by both sides, and a corresponding shift in attention from social and economic issues to allegations of maltreatment by the security forces, culminating in the Lower Falls curfew of July 1970 and the internment and interrogation operation of August 1971. This was accompanied by the rebirth of militant Republicanism and organised guerrilla activity by persons whose main objective was not social and economic reform but the pursuit of Irish nationalism and the abolition of partition. This process and the response of the legal system to it is traced in the next chapter.

Continued support for the various protests and demonstrations

16

from which these confrontations developed, and even sympathy for the guerrilla activists who eventually emerged, was nonetheless dependent on the persistent feeling among members of the minority community that their social and economic rights were being denied. It is important therefore to consider why the reform programme failed to win the confidence of those whom it was intended to benefit.

The Failure of the Reform Programme to Win the Confidence of the Minority

The principal factor in this was perhaps the long delay in the implementation of the reform of local government. The fierce political battle between the two wings of the Unionist Party over this issue gave substance to the view that the Unionists would not willingly grant any reforms which would be any more than token gestures.

A number of leading Catholics, for instance, issued a statement in September 1971, following the internment operation, questioning whether any Unionist government could be entrusted with the introduction and implementation of a reform programme, and alleging that 'the continued application of the Brookeborough formula of government by discrimination was maintaining intact the Unionist position of power'.[10] It is easy to understand this feeling, given that the Unionist Party at that time was still in control of a number of local authority councils though its supporters were clearly a minority of the electorate, and that arrangements for a completely new and patently fair system would not be ready for implementation until 1973. The only action which had been taken in this field in the two years following the violence of 1968 and 1969 was the replacement of the patently gerrymandered Londonderry Corporation by a non-elected Commission. Though the work of the Commission was generally praised, it remained a fact that control over local government was still denied to the elected representatives of the Roman Catholic community in areas where they were clearly in a majority.

17

A similar point may be made in relation to the reform of public housing. This had always been one of the most emotional issues in the civil rights campaign. Unionist councils, it was alleged, reserved the bulk of the better new houses for their own supporters. The validity of this claim has been contested on a statistical basis on the ground that overall the Catholic community did obtain a larger proportional share of public housing resources than the Protestant community, but more detailed analysis of the housing and census returns suggests that in Unionist controlled areas Protestants were given a disproportionate share of new houses.[11] The Cameron Commission concluded that there had been discrimination:

> We have no doubt . . ., in the light of the mass of evidence put before us, that in these Unionist-controlled areas it was fairly frequent for housing policy to be operated so that houses allocated to Catholics tended . . . to go to rehouse slum dwellers, whereas Protestant allocations tended to go more frequently to new families.[12]

Nor can it be doubted that some Unionist controlled local councils did make use of their control over housing to perpetuate their electoral advantage by allocating their own supporters in such a way as to maintain control over marginal wards, and ensuring that their more numerous opponents were safely gathered together in one or two predominantly Roman Catholic estates. The Cameron Commission concluded:

> Council housing policy has also been distorted for political ends in the Unionist controlled areas. . . . In each, houses have been built and allocated in such a way that they will not disturb the political balance.[13]

The strategy for reform in housing was one of centralisation. In terms of administrative convenience and efficiency, and of staffing in an increasingly specialised profession, this policy can scarcely be contested. And although there was the expected delay in implementing the plan, so that the new central Housing Executive did not begin to take over the public housing functions of local councils until 1972, the proposed scheme was broadly welcomed in all quarters. In the meantime a fair points system was to be operated in all districts, though the spirit of the scheme was not always adhered to.[14] But once again the net effect of centralisation was to leave the balance of control over housing allocation in the hands of the representatives of the majority community who naturally outnumbered those of the minority on the new central authority. This is not to say that the new central agency was guilty of improper practices or discriminatory allocation. But at the lower levels of administration many of the old familiar faces continued to confront those who applied for new or exchanged tenancies, and the local representatives of the Roman Catholic community were until May 1973 no more in control in Roman Catholic areas than ever they were.

The Ombudsmen

It is in this context of continuing control of local government in most areas by the established Unionist Councils that the performance of other less far-reaching elements in the reform programme should be judged. Ombudsmen with wide powers to scrutinise the decisions of both central and local government agencies had been promised in the initial reform packages of November 1968 and September 1969 respectively. The Northern Ireland Parliamentary Commissioner of Administration covering central government, and the Commissioner for Complaints, a similar office in respect of local government, were appointed without undue delay in July 1969 and December 1969 respectively and went to work immediately on a large number of outstanding complaints. Reports on their first completed investigations followed soon after. But in neither case did the new system make much impact, and there were no forthright revelations of the kinds of blatant discrimination which the Roman Catholic community had come to believe were widespread.

There were a number of factors which may help to explain this lack of impact. In the first place the actual extent of blatant discrimination had been somewhat exaggerated. Both the Parliamentary Commissioner and the Commissioner for Complaints reported favourably on the generally high standard of administration in central and local government. Furthermore many of the most publicised cases of imbalance between Unionist and non-

Unionist representatives on public bodies and in senior civil service posts could be attributed to the disinclination of some Roman Catholics in earlier years to become involved in the institutions of a state to which they preferred not to give their recognition and support. In the second place, the Commissioners were barred by their terms of reference from doing anything about cases of discrimination which arose from decisions made prior to the establishment of their offices. Nor were they in a position to do anything about established patterns of discrimination, in particular in local government employment and housing. Their terms of reference were directed to the scrutiny of individual decisions rather than the overall percentages of employees or housing allocations among members of the two religious and political communities. Even in respect of current decisions it was, in any case, virtually impossible to establish conclusively that improper factors had been taken into account given the accepted tradition of tacit understanding in matters of this kind in Northern Ireland. The Commissioner for Complaints commented openly in his second report on the difficulty of obtaining information about the numbers of Protestants and Roman Catholics employed in the bodies with which he was concerned.[15]

In any event the Commissioners failed to reveal any noteworthy cases of discrimination in the early years of their work. And yet there were a number of highly publicised cases of just the kind of apparently blatant discrimination with which the new agencies were intended to deal – notably over the non-appointment of a Mr Doherty to a post with the Londonderry Commission on the direction of the Ministry of Development.[16]

Finally, and perhaps most important, the Commissioners were debarred from dealing with cases of discrimination at the most serious political level. For instance, in the widely publicised case of a decision by a Protestant Rural District Council to refuse permission to the local Roman Catholic Gaelic League to make use of the Council's playing fields for their traditional Sunday matches, the Commissioner held that he could not in the absence of any procedural irregularities consider the merits of the decision itself. Similarly, the Commissioner felt himself debarred from interfering in cases where the allegation was of communal rather than individual discrimination. In one publicised case concerning the alleged failure of a local authority to provide health and welfare facilities in a predominantly Roman Catholic area, the Commissioner informed the complainant that 'The Act under which he operated . . . was intended essentially to provide a means whereby the complaints of an individual citizen who felt he had been unfairly treated by a local or public authority could be investigated; it was not intended to deal with issues affecting equally the whole general public in a large area'.[17] Yet it was precisely this kind of large-scale discrimination which had been central to the allegations of the civil rights campaigners.

It is thus scarcely surprising that the activists in the minority community refused to believe that they could expect any real assistance from the new agencies. The Commissioners did have some measure of success in dealing with minor cases of administrative tangles and insensitivity, in which their intervention was crucial to the working out of a satisfactory settlement; but their political impact was minimal. Whether this was due to a lack of zeal in rooting out the real reasons underlying contested decisions and relentlessly pursuing any matters raised to the limit of their express powers, or to a defect in the formulation of the powers and duties of the new agencies, must remain a matter of opinion. But it would be difficult to argue convincingly that the new ombudsmen performed the job that they were ostensibly appointed to do.

The Police

A similar comment may be made in respect of the structural reform of the police. Following the recommendations of the Hunt Report in October 1968, the paramilitary B Specials were disbanded and replaced by the part-time Ulster Defence Regiment under British Army command. The Royal Ulster Constabulary was also to be reconstituted as a wholly civilian and non-armed force on the British model under the control of a widely representative Police Authority. The continuing violence and the growth of guerrilla activity effectively thwarted the

21

achievement of the first objective. And the new Police Authority failed to assert itself in such a way as to alter the public conception of the police force as an agent of the Unionist Government. In one of its early decisions on the highly emotive question of marching, the Authority was equally divided on a decision to ban a particular march. The Chairman who had the casting vote suggested that instead of using it the decision should be referred back to the Minister of Home Affairs. This was accepted. Here again the reform programme, whatever its intentions, clearly failed to achieve any change in public attitudes to established institutions.

Subsequent Civil Rights Cases

Two further cases of a civil rights character which were finally pursued in the courts should also be mentioned. Both originated in Dungannon under the general auspices of the Campaign for Social Justice. The first was brought against the Dungannon RDC in respect of alleged discrimination in the allocation of houses on a new council estate. The case came before Mr Justice Gibson early in 1971. On any objective assessment his judgment on the case could only be taken as a qualified victory for the complainants: 'The failure of the defendants to allot a proportion only of the houses to incoming workers, the enlargement of that class beyond its legitimate bounds and the priority of allocation given to them would operate to reduce the number of houses available to other applicants to a degree which could cause considerable hardship in some cases and constitutes an illegitimate operation of the [points] scheme.' And he gave an informal direction to the Council to consider the allocation of the disputed houses 'in accordance with the principles which he had stated rather than in the manner in which they had hitherto acted'.[18] Nonetheless, the introduction to his reasoned judgment was one-sided:

> Before becoming involved in the details of the case, I think I should state at the outset my clear conclusion that the evidence of such lettings as were considered did not at all indicate that the Defendants selected tenants for houses in a capricious way

or from motives of discrimination, or that the applications of persons who were not supporters of the Unionist majority in the Council suffered by having their claims deliberately deferred or overlooked.

This stated only part of the final conclusion to the case. The evidence did not establish impropriety; nor did it establish that there was no impropriety. It was this introduction which caused the local press to report that the judge had cleared the Council of any impropriety. This may have been influential in the decision not to take the case further.

The second case was brought against the Dungannon Urban District Council over the failure to pursue a redevelopment scheme in the way suggested by a Ministry inspector allegedly with the object of injuring local Roman Catholic business opportunities. Here too the case came before Mr Justice Gibson in April 1971, and was rejected on the ground that the issue could not be decided on affidavit evidence alone, prior to the trial of the case on the evidence of relevant witnesses. Whether the evidence of witnesses would have been sufficient was never tested, since the case was not pursued further.

Conclusion

A number of comments may be made on these cases in particular, and on the legal response to the civil rights campaign in general. First, it is doubtful whether the British style of legal decision-making, in which cases were dealt with on the basis of very precise and often highly technical points rather than the broad issues underlying the dispute, was appropriate in civil rights litigation. This approach was perhaps more attractive to the judges, in that it enabled them to sidestep the main issues. But all too often it meant that the courts did not fulfil their main function of dealing with those main issues in so far as they were subject to legal adjudication. When the guarantors of civil rights take refuge in technicalities, aggrieved complainants are more likely to take to the streets.

In the second place the judges were unwilling to make the kind of condemnation of unlawful or improper practices which in simple terms would hit the headlines. Even in cases which were effectively won, as in the first Dungannon case, the careful language of the judgment permitted the decision to be portrayed as a vindication of the errant defendant. Public confidence in the courts as the ultimate and impartial guarantors of freedom and justice within the law requires a much more open approach to speech writing than was traditional in British legal circles. It is notable that after the introduction of internment, the judiciary did adopt a much more forceful stance on civil liberties, and public confidence increased accordingly. But any beneficial effect was lost by the superimposition of extra-legal powers, as discussed in detail in chapter 7.

A similar comment may be made about the work of the new anti-discrimination agencies. Neither the Parliamentary Commissioner nor the Commissioner for Complaints was prepared to make the kind of forthright condemnation of Unionist power structures which the minority wanted. Some of the factors which lay behind this failure have already been discussed. But the low-key style in which the Commissioners approached their work was perhaps as important as any of the more formal restraints imposed on them by their terms of reference. The obligation imposed on the Commissioners to preserve complete confidentiality in their investigations and reports was clearly a crucial factor in this context. But there is no indication that this was an unwelcome restriction in the eyes of those concerned. The pace and language of the British civil service tradition which was consistently followed by the Commissioners was as inappropriate as the technicality of the British legal system as a means of building up confidence in the organs of government in a divided community.

These criticisms of the courts and the new ombudsmen, however, must be set in the broader context of the situation in Northern Ireland. Discrimination was a structural problem created over a period of many years of decision-making affecting both individual job appointments and the allocation of public resources. The imbalance in the proportion of Roman Catholics and Protestants in senior civil service and local government posts could not have been corrected overnight by any form of judicial or quasi-judicial supervision or control. Nor could major decisions taken in the past, such as the siting of the New University in Coleraine rather than Londonderry, allegedly for political rather than academic reasons, or the concentration of economic development in the predominantly Protestant area east of the River Bann (though here there were probably more apparently valid though politically shortsighted reasons for the decision), be corrected by judicial review alone even if they had been open to independent scrutiny. No amount of civil rights litigation or review could of itself have solved the problems created by political bias. Nonetheless the courts and later the ombudsmen failed to bring these issues into the open in such a way as to assist in the political reform process.

NOTES AND REFERENCES

1. *Disturbances in Northern Ireland* Cmd. 532, Belfast 1969, para. 229.
2. *Constitutional Law in Northern Ireland* by Harry Calvert, 1968, pp. 334–335.
3. For a further description of the attempts to seek redress in the courts by the Campaign for Social Justice, see 'The Search for Justice in Northern Ireland' by W. Don Carroll *New York University Journal of International Law and Politics,* Vol. 6, Spring 1973.
4. *Fortnight* No. 17, 14 May 1971.
5. See for example, *In Search of Justice* by Brian Abel Smith and Robert Stevens, 1968, Chapter 6.
6. For example, there have been surprising changes in judicial attitudes on the part of judges appointed to the United States Supreme Court.
7. The ban was lifted in March 1973.
8. *McEldowney v. Forde* [1969] 3 W.L.R. 179.
9. *Northern Ireland: Text of a Communique and Declaration issued after a meeting held at 10 Downing Street on August 19th 1969* Cmnd. 4154, London 1969.
10. *Commentary upon the White Paper (Command Paper 558) entitled 'A Record of Constructive Change'* Belfast 1971.
11. See *Governing Without Consensus* by Richard Rose, 1971, and the criticisms of it in *Housing in Northern Ireland* by W. D. Birrell *et al.,* Centre for Environmental Studies, University Working Paper 12, 1971, p. 149.
12. Cmd. 532, para. 140.
13. Cmd. 532, para. 139.
14. In his annual report for 1972 the Commissioner for Complaints referred to three cases of maladministration of housing allocation by a local authority in which 'the members, on the last occasion on which they were in a position to exercise powers of allocation under the

Housing Acts, appeared to have decided to have a "last fling"'. H.C. 158, Belfast 1973, para. 31.

15. *Second Report of the Northern Ireland Commissioner for Complaints* H.C. 2048, Belfast 1970, para. 53.
16. *Fortnight* No. 9, 22 January 1971.
17. *Fortnight* No. 10, 5 February 1971.
18. *Fortnight* No. 14, 2 April 1971, *Campbell & Casey v. Dungannon RDC*, 19 March 1971.

3. FROM CIVIL RIGHTS TO GUERRILLA WARFARE

The slide from peaceful protest into guerrilla warfare in Northern Ireland was a gradual process which stretched from the summer of 1968 up to the introduction of internment in August 1971. As the process continued there was a corresponding change in the primary focus of attention from civil rights to law and order, from protection from discrimination to protection from physical violence by terrorists or security forces. The legal response to these new problems, however, was no more successful than to those of discrimination. The rest of this study is an attempt to explain this failure of law and lawyers to stem the descent into communal and military conflict. Before dealing with the specifically legal issues which were raised in this phase of the Northern Ireland crisis a brief general account will be given of the background to the slide into violence and terrorism. Three major factors can perhaps be isolated by way of explanation.

The first was the build up of a sense of frustration in the Roman Catholic community at the failure of their attempts to achieve any real progress by political agitation alone. Significantly this feeling of frustration was particularly strong in Londonderry, where serious violence first broke out. Following the recession of 1965 a newly founded and government-assisted factory closed down, throwing some 2000 men out of work. With the continuing decline in the traditional textile and shirt-making industry this raised the unemployment rate in the city to more than 10 per cent. About the same time the final decisions were made to move the county administrative offices from Londonderry, the natural capital, to the predominantly Protestant centre of Coleraine in the east of the county, and to establish the proposed New University of Ulster there. These three decisions were seen

27

as final proof that the Unionist Government was prepared to jettison Londonderry, which despite its significance in Orange history could not be 'held' indefinitely given the two to one majority of Roman Catholics in the population. All this occurred in a period when for the first time the Nationalist Party had decided to take an active part in local government. Similar feeling in other centres, like Dungannon and Newry and West Belfast, where active political representation by a new generation of capable non-Unionist MPs had likewise failed to produce any substantial results, set the scene for the mass support for the initial peaceful marches and demonstrations and later for more militant action and rioting. As none of the allegedly discriminatory decisions which were contested during this period were later altered, this feeling of frustration continued throughout the period of emergency.

The second factor was the increasingly violent reaction in the Protestant community to the civil rights campaign. For a long time this was centred on the colourful but supposedly irrelevant antics of Ian Paisley and his band of religious and political supporters, though there had been flare-ups of more serious sectarian violence, notably in the Malvern Street murder affair of 1966 and the Cromac Square and Divis Street disturbances in Belfast. But as the civil rights campaign moved into the phase of public demonstrations and protests the determination of the Protestant militants to interfere with civil rights marches and meetings, and where possible to prevent their occurrence, became more and more apparent. Attacks were made by Protestant extremists on civil rights supporters in Dungannon in August, November and December 1968, in Armagh in November 1968 and in Londonderry in January 1969, as recorded in the report of the Cameron Commission.

The official response of the Unionist government, under the direction of the Minister of Home Affairs, William Craig, to the civil rights campaign was likewise openly repressive. A blanket ban on Republican clubs in any form had been introduced under the Special Powers Act at the very beginning of the active phase of the civil rights campaign, though this was as much a symbolic as a real measure of oppression. More practically, the government adopted an increasingly restrictive attitude to civil rights demonstrations and marches. Marches and counter-marches were a long standing problem in Northern Ireland, and the authorities had wide powers under both the Public Order Acts and the Special Powers Act to control the route of proposed marches or to ban them altogether. The necessity for some power to control demonstrations could scarcely be contested given the practice among opponents of any particular faction of organising or threatening an opposing march or demonstration on the same route. But equally, it can hardly be doubted that in the early phases of the civil rights campaign the powers were used in a partisan fashion.

The most notorious example of this was the banning of the civil rights march proposed for October 1968 in Londonderry because an allegedly traditional Apprentice Boys parade was threatened. The Cameron Commission found this to have been devised specially for the occasion.[1] The net effect in the opinion of the Cameron Commission was an increase in support for the march and in the militancy of many of the marchers. But it was undoubtedly the violent attack by the police on the marchers, widely recorded on television and by the press, which finally convinced the people of Derry that the government was committed to a policy of repression rather than reform.

From then on it became increasingly difficult to distinguish between official and unofficial reactionary violence, at least for the Roman Catholic community. Large numbers of the 'B Special' constabulary were undoubtedly involved, though in a private capacity, in the organised ambush on the People's Democracy march from Belfast to Londonderry at Burntollet in January 1969. The ensuing riotous confrontations in Londonderry in January and April were followed by two night-time 'invasions' of the Roman Catholic Bogside area by large numbers of uniformed RUC officers in the course of which substantial damage and injury to residents and property was inflicted. Final confirmation for the minority community of the unity of purpose between the RUC, the B Specials and the Protestant militants was given by the events of August 1969 in Londonderry, Armagh, Coalisland, Dungannon, Dungiven and Belfast, which eventually led to the deployment of British troops. Detailed analysis of these events is beyond the scope of this study. The report of the

Scarman Tribunal concluded that the RUC was in the main a non-partisan force caught between two sets of militants bent on violent confrontation, a victim of circumstances and its own faulty intelligence, rather than a willing participant in the violence.[2] But it is a fact that the RUC failed to prevent large numbers of houses on the fringes of Roman Catholic areas in Belfast from being burnt out. And the action of the few 'black sheep' in the force and the failure of their superior officers either to control them in advance or to discipline them after the event reduced still further the confidence of the minority in the impartiality of the RUC.

The third factor was the growing conflict between British troops and the Provisional IRA. This was a seemingly inexorable and self-perpetuating process. British troops were brought in to act as peace-keepers between the two communities in August 1969, when the local police and the B Specials could no longer contain the situation. The arrival of the soldiers was widely welcomed by the Roman Catholic community as a guarantee against further Protestant attacks. But Army commanders were aware that their men were not trained or suited for a long-term peace-keeping role, and issued frequent statements on the need for a political solution. These fears proved amply justified. It is now widely accepted that in the summer of 1969 the IRA existed as a serious military force only in the files of the RUC Special Branch, and in the imagination of leading Unionist politicians.[3] The development of genuine guerrilla potential and of the will to take on the British Army was the result of a series of political and military blunders by the British, and of support and encouragement from traditional Republican activists from the South.

The first moves to rebuild the IRA were almost wholly defensive.[4] Emissaries were sent to Dublin in the late summer of 1969 to seek assistance for the protection of the Roman Catholic enclaves in Belfast. They were given both arms and money, some of it diverted under highly disputed circumstances from the official government funds voted by the Dail for the relief of those who had suffered in the North.[5] Local defence groups and vigilante forces were set up to man the barricades, and prepare for any new onslaughts. Senior Army officers were careful to keep up a direct line of communication with these

30

groups in the months that followed the British intervention. But as the exasperation of the ordinary soldiers increased at the endless confrontations and riots, whose underlying causes they could not understand, and the pressures from Unionist politicians for a tougher Army line with rioters grew, so the downward spiral of antagonism between soldiers and the Roman Catholic communities in Londonderry and Belfast gathered pace.

At the start there were minor incidents of verbal abuse and harassment, especially in the case of those Scottish regiments which were regarded as particularly partial to the Protestant cause. Increasingly the stones and bottles of the rioters were replaced by petrol bombs and grenades, and the batons and barbed wire of the soldiers by CS gas and rubber bullets. The confrontation reached disastrous proportions in the Lower Falls curfew of July 1970, which followed almost accidentally from a routine arms search. Then there were the first fatal shooting of a rioter, the killing of Daniel O'Hagan in the New Lodge Road area of Belfast in 1970, and the first Army fatality at the hands of the IRA in February 1971. During the spring and summer of 1971 the Provisional IRA activists encouraged and organised young rioters in Ballymurphy and the Bogside and then moved in with weapons and explosives themselves, in the hope of provoking the soldiers into unjustifiable action, which could then be used as justification for further confrontations. This policy was extremely successful. The fatal shootings of Beattie and Cusack in Londonderry in July 1971 in circumstances which gave some justification to the Army, but not enough to silence the demands for an inquiry, led to the withdrawal of the opposition party from the Stormont Parliament and thus to the failure of the policy of pressing for a political settlement by gradual means.

By this time the Provisional IRA had clearly built itself into a strong and well-organised military force with a fair measure of tacit support in the main Roman Catholic enclaves. The introduction of internment in August 1971 completed the process. The list of those arrested and detained was so out-of-date and haphazard, and the treatment meted out in the detention and interrogation centres, as reported by the Compton Tribunal[6] and in subsequent legal proceedings, was so harsh as to unite the Roman Catholic community in Northern Ireland behind the

IRA as never before. Recruitment and financial support are reported to have risen dramatically on both sides of the border, and the phase of all-out guerrilla warfare began in earnest. In the seven months prior to the introduction of internment in August 1971, twelve soldiers were killed; from September to December in that year forty members of the security forces were killed. The initial reaction to internment was reinforced by continuing Army harassment and arrests in the Roman Catholic areas and by a series of disputed incidents in which allegedly innocent civilians were shot by Army patrols.

The most significant of these incidents was the shooting dead of thirteen civilians by paratroops in Londonderry on 'Bloody Sunday', 29 January 1972. The national and international concern expressed over this incident and the widespread feeling that the resulting public inquiry exonerating those responsible had been 'widgered' brought a new urgency to British government policy on Northern Ireland. At the end of March 1972 the Stormont parliament was suspended, when the Northern Ireland premier, Brian Faulkner, refused to hand over formal control of internal security to Westminster. 'Direct rule' from London was immediately imposed. The new Secretary of State for Northern Ireland, William Whitelaw, at first sought to engineer a political settlement with representatives of the IRA. But when the brief cease-fire which had been arranged broke down in July 1972, it was decided to turn the full force of the British Army against the IRA. The 'no-go' areas which had been established in Londonderry and certain parts of Belfast, and from which the IRA had been organising its bombing and shooting campaign, were overrun by troops in Operation Motorman in August 1972. This was followed by the introduction in November 1972 of a new system for the arrest and detention of suspected terrorists under the Detention of Terrorists Order 1972. The number of persons detained without trial, which had reached a peak of some 900 under the Unionist regime and then declined to some 250 during the search for a negotiated settlement, rose sharply during the first half of 1973 to more than 500 as the Army built up its own security operation in militant Republican areas. This new policy was successful in the sense that there was a continuing decline in the number of shooting incidents involving the security forces and terrorists. But the level of bomb attacks on civilian and military targets did not show a similar decline, and at the end of 1974 both the Provisional IRA and the British Army were still pursuing their mutual war with determination and zeal, despite the arrest and detention of large numbers of leading IRA commanders and officers.

The imposition of direct rule also led to a resurgence of organised paramilitary activity on the Protestant side. Both the Ulster Defence Association (UDA) and the Ulster Volunteer Force (UVF) soon became involved in a campaign of assassination and bombing against Roman Catholic civilians and premises. Sectarian assassinations reached a peak in the autumn of 1972 and then gradually declined,[7] but were resumed again in the aftermath of the IRA assassination of a judge and a magistrate in September 1974. These activities led in their turn to the imposition of Army security operations in certain Protestant areas and the internment of a number of suspected Protestant terrorists.

There was a similar resurgence of militant Protestant feeling in the political sphere. Direct rule was followed by a series of short political strikes which brought industry and commerce in many parts of the province to a halt. The culmination of these was the Ulster Workers Council strike in May 1974 which brought down the 'power-sharing' government of moderate Unionists and the main Roman Catholic party, the SDLP. This government had been painstakingly put together by William Whitelaw following the proportional representation elections held in June 1973 under the new Northern Ireland Constitution Act, but had failed to bring the major part of Protestant opinion along with it in the search for a longer term structure for relationships between Northern Ireland and the Republic. Thus at the end of 1974 Northern Ireland was left in a situation similar to that prevailing at its creation, with the vast majority of both Protestants and Roman Catholics giving their support to political parties which sought to give effect to mutually incompatible aspirations. The Protestant community still demanded the continuation of a specifically non-Irish state in Northern Ireland, while the Roman Catholic community sought a settlement which looked towards the ultimate unification of Northern

Ireland with the Republic.

Various explanations may be offered for this progression of events. One factor was the failure of the programmes for social and economic reform to bring about any marked change in conditions in the Roman Catholic enclaves where the Provisional IRA gained its support. Another was the failure of the British and Irish governments to find a political formula which provided a sound base for the resumption of ordinary democratic government in Northern Ireland in which both Protestants and Roman Catholics were content to participate. But the most important was perhaps the failure of government to find a satisfactory method of dealing with public disorder and terrorism. It is this third factor with which the ensuing chapters are primarily concerned. But some general comments on the part played by the British Army in the period from 1969 when soldiers first appeared on the streets in Londonderry and Belfast to the end of 1974 may help to set the security operation in a more general context.

There was always the danger that the close proximity of troops and civilians in the rougher areas of Belfast and Londonderry would lead to trouble. In the Ballymurphy area of Belfast and the Bogside of Londonderry, where most of the initial confrontations took place in the course of 1970 and 1971, it was not long before the friendly tea-sipping days of the soldiers' initial reception gave way to accusations of unnecessary force being used in dealing with riotous youngsters. The soldiers in turn began to lose patience with the numerous conflicting roles which they were called on to perform, from social welfare and youth work to the control of riots. The risk that the minor confrontations which naturally developed would escalate into a more serious conflict was obvious, and was openly recognised by Army commanders in the early stages of the operation. But little was done to prevent the process from developing.

In the first place senior Army officers and politicians failed to appreciate fully either the frustrations and fears of the Roman Catholic community, or the developing antagonism between ordinary soldiers and the civilians whose streets they were patrolling. The situation was especially confusing for the soldier on the ground. He did not have an identifiable enemy and was confronted daily by people of the same class as himself who spoke

34

the same language, but who at one time in the day would be quite friendly and at another would throw stones and bottles at him. This problem became particularly acute when, as a result of political pressure both from the Unionist and later from the new Tory government in Britain, the Army began to take a tougher attitude towards rioting and to intensify their search for arms and explosives in Roman Catholic areas without at the same time undertaking similar searches in Protestant areas. This inevitably led to ill-feeling between individual soldiers and the large numbers of innocent people whose houses were 'ransacked' or who were subjected to inconvenience and harassment, as for instance in the Lower Falls curfew operation in July 1970.

In the second place the nature of the Army as a closed institution unaccustomed to direct contact with the civilian population increased the likelihood that individual soldiers would be guilty of misconduct.[8] The standard weapons and procedures of the Army were inappropriate both for the task of crowd and riot control and for the conduct of arrest and search operations. Individual soldiers knew that there was a major propaganda campaign to show how effectively they were dealing with the situation and soon realised that any breaches of discipline would be concealed by their colleagues or condoned by their officers. This applied both to minor incidents in which soldiers manhandled those whom they were arresting or damaged premises in which they were carrying out searches and also to more serious shooting incidents in which civilians were deliberately or accidentally shot. The monolithic and bureaucratic nature of the Army ensured that a major effort would be made to see that any soldier accused of misconduct while on duty would be cleared of any allegations or charges brought against him. As a result the public, and especially the population in the main Roman Catholic areas, soon came to believe that there was no chance of obtaining justice in any case involving the Army.

The contribution of these various factors to the downward spiral of confrontation and conflict could be plotted in detail in a day to day, or month by month account of events in Northern Ireland from 1969 to 1974. The main concern of the chapters which follow, however, is the more limited one of explaining the failure of the legal system to act as a brake on the escalation of

35

violence between the Army and the IRA by providing an acceptable means of dealing with terrorism by legal means.

NOTES AND REFERENCES

1. *Disturbances in Northern Ireland* Cmd. 532, Belfast 1969, para. 160.
2. *Violence and Civil Disturbances in Northern Ireland in 1969* Cmd. 566, Belfast 1972, Chapter 3.
3. Cmd. 566, Chapter 3.8.
4. For a full account of the rebirth of the IRA, see *Ulster* by The Sunday Times Insight Team, 1972.
5. See the report of the Public Accounts Committee set up by the Parliament of the Republic of Ireland, P.R.L. 2574, Dublin 1972.
6. *Report of the enquiry into allegations against the security forces of physical brutality in Northern Ireland arising out of events on the 9th August, 1971,* Cmnd. 4823, London 1971.
7. For a full account see *Political Murder in Northern Ireland* by Martin Dillon and Denis Lehane, 1973.
8. This point is taken from an unpublished submission by Gill Boehringer to the Parker Committee on methods of interrogation.

4. EMERGENCY POWERS: ARREST AND SCREENING

The main focus of public concern over police and Army operations in the course of the emergency in Northern Ireland was not the extent of the powers granted to them but their alleged abuse in individual incidents. From the initial police assault on the civil rights marchers in Londonderry in October 1968 and the ensuing police incursions into the Bogside there was a continual series of allegations of misconduct, of unlawful physical assaults and beatings, and even of deliberate assassinations on the part of the security forces. The response of the authorities to such allegations and to the various political and legal actions taken by the complainants is discussed in chapter 7 in the context of a more general assessment of the factors affecting public confidence in the legal system. The purpose of this chapter is to explain the formal basis of police and Army powers in Northern Ireland both under the Special Powers Act and the Northern Ireland (Emergency Provisions) Act and to describe how these powers were used in practice.

The Special Powers Act

Until 1973 the basis of police and Army operations against terrorists, and to a lesser extent against public disorder, was the Civil Authorities (Special Powers) Act (Northern Ireland) 1922–1933, commonly known as the Special Powers Act, and the numerous regulations made under it. As has already been explained, this body of law was originally introduced as a temporary measure to replace the provisions of the Restoration of Order in

Ireland Act 1920, which the government in London was not prepared to allow to be enforced in any part of Ireland in view of the political settlement with the Southern Irish leaders. It therefore suggested to the Northern Unionists that they should make their own emergency arrangements for the restoration of order. The Special Powers Act was re-enacted from year to year until 1933 and was then rendered permanent. It conferred wide powers of arrest, questioning, search, detention and internment on the police and troops as agents of the Ministry of Home Affairs, and gave almost completely unrestricted power to the Minister to make regulations with the force of law. Many such regulations were made: for instance, to proscribe certain organisations, to regulate the conduct of parades and funerals and to make detailed provision for long-term detention or internment.

The Special Powers Act was directed and used almost exclusively against Republican activists,[1] at least until the imposition of direct rule from London in 1972, and its repeal was high on the list of demands expressed during the civil rights campaign. But it was always regarded as more or less unchallengeable in the courts. In an early case arising out of the arrest and detention in 1922 of a prosperous hotel owner in Portadown who was allegedly involved in a conspiracy against the state, a charge which was vigorously denied, the Northern Ireland High Court rejected an application for *habeas corpus* on the ground that under the Act it was within the power of the Minister of Home Affairs to make what detention and internment orders he thought fit and that it was not for the Court to express an opinion on the facts of the case.[2] It has been argued that this decision was incorrect, notably in the second edition of Halsbury's Statutes, on the ground that an objective assessment of the facts was required under the terms of the Act and that the matter could therefore be inquired into by the courts.[3] But the futility of making any such challenge to ministerial decisions under the Act was effectively confirmed by the outcome of the Republican Clubs case, as described in chapter 2. After the introduction of internment in August 1971 a number of successful test cases were mounted in the courts on the grounds of certain procedural and constitutional irregularities, as discussed in detail in chapter 7. Many of the arrests made in the initial arrest operation in August 1971, for instance, were held to have been unlawful on the ground that those exercising the emergency powers under the Act had nonetheless to fulfil the ordinary common law requirement of informing the person arrested of the ground for the arrest.[4] As this had not always been clearly done, a formal re-arrest had to be made in a substantial number of cases and damages were eventually paid to those concerned in respect of their technically unlawful detention.[5] But there were no cases in which the effective release of a person detained or interned under the Special Powers Act was secured by legal action.

The Northern Ireland (Emergency Provisions) Act 1973

When full control of internal security in Northern Ireland was taken over by the Westminster government in the spring of 1972 one of the first political priorities of the new regime was the repeal of the Special Powers Act, and its replacement by a more generally acceptable structure for dealing with terrorists. The task of making recommendations to this effect was entrusted to a committee chaired by Lord Diplock, though provision for a new system of detention without trial was in fact made by an Order in Council in November 1972 before the Diplock Committee finally reported.[6]

The main concern of the Diplock Committee in so far as powers of arrest and questioning were concerned was to simplify the formal procedures for arrest and detention and so to avoid the problems which had arisen under the somewhat complex provisions of the Special Powers Act, particularly where arrests were made by legally inexperienced soldiers rather than policemen. The Committee recommended that members of the armed forces should have power to arrest without warrant any person suspected of involvement in or having information about terrorist offences and to detain him for up to four hours for the purpose of establishing his identity (para. 49).[7] The ground for this recommendation, as stated by the Committee, was as follows:

39

It is, we think, preposterous to expect a young soldier making an arrest under these conditions to be able to identify a person whom he has arrested as being a man whom he knows to be wanted for a particular offence so as to be able to inform him accurately of the grounds on which he is arresting him. It is impossible to question arrested persons on the spot to establish their identity. In practice this cannot usually be ascertained until they have been taken to the safety of battalion headquarters. Even here it may be a lengthy process, as suspects often give false names or addresses or giving their true names, which are often very common ones, assert that some relation or other person of the same name is the real person who is wanted for a particular offence. It is only when his identity has been satisfactorily established that it is possible to be reasonably certain of the particular ground on which he was liable to arrest and to inform him of it (para. 45).

The Committee also recommended that it should be an offence to refuse to answer or to give a false or misleading answer to any question reasonably put by a member of the security forces in this context (para. 49).

These recommendations were broadly followed in the Northern Ireland (Emergency Provisions) Act which was finally enacted in July 1973. The Act gave the Army power to arrest and detain for up to four hours any person suspected of terrorist activity (s. 12). At the end of that period the person had to be either released or handed over to the police for formal charging or for a further period of questioning up to a limit of seventy-two hours (s. 10). Both the Army and the police were also given a further power to stop and question any person as to his identity and knowledge of terrorist incidents (s. 16). These provisions were rather more tightly drawn than had been suggested in the Diplock Committee report, in that arrest for questioning was restricted to those persons who were themselves suspected of involvement in terrorist activities, and in that no power was granted for the explicit purpose of arresting and questioning persons suspected merely of knowledge of terrorist activities.

These minor changes in drafting, however, made little practical difference. Both the Special Powers Act and the Northern Ireland (Emergency Provisions) Act constituted an effective abrogation of the rule of law in the sense that under them the security authorities retained the power to arrest and detain anyone they pleased without having to give any justification and without fear of being called to account in respect of any decisions later shown to have been unjustified. To that extent Northern Ireland had always been and remained a permanent potential police state.

In addition it should be remembered that where action under the emergency legislation was legally doubtful or politically unattractive, the security forces could always fall back on the common law. The curfew which was imposed in the Lower Falls area of Belfast in July 1970 was subsequently justified in a test case brought against one of those who had not observed the restrictions proclaimed by the Army commander: the magistrate who heard the case held that the commander was entitled at common law to make what orders were necessary for the preservation of the peace in an emergency situation.[8] The lack of clarity and precision in the common law rules in such cases and the knowledge on the part of the security forces that the courts would be likely to take a sympathetic view if a legal case were brought against them added to the freedom of action already conferred on them by the emergency legislation.

Military Security and Police Prosecution

The removal of normal legal controls on the exercise of powers of arrest and search meant that both the Army and the police were free to organise their security operations in whatever way they pleased. The policies and practice of the various branches of the police and Army were accordingly guided and controlled more by their own internal constraints and values than by the provisions of the law.

Before the British Army became deeply involved in security operations this fact was most clearly demonstrated by the difference in approach between the Special Branch and the ordinary criminal investigation branch of the Royal Ulster Constabulary. The Special Branch maintained lists of active or supposedly active Republicans whom they were prepared to arrest and detain whenever the political or security situation appeared to call for it, as for instance during the IRA campaign of 1956 to 1962 and on the outbreak of violence in Belfast in August 1969. The ordinary criminal investigation detectives on the other hand would only seek to arrest and detain a person whom they suspected of having committed a crime.

As the Army became more deeply involved in internal security in Northern Ireland it gradually took over this 'special branch' role from the police. The army established its own under-cover security branch after the obvious failure of the RUC Special Branch to identify the most dangerous and active terrorists for the purposes of the initial internment operation of August 1971. And when direct rule was imposed early in 1972 and the new system of detention was introduced later in the year, the Army developed an entirely independent security policy based on what was to become its four-hour power of arrest and interrogation under the Emergency Provisions Act. A large-scale 'screening' operation was undertaken in the main Roman Catholic areas with a view to finding out more precisely who was and who was not involved in or sympathetic to IRA activities. In the course of this large numbers of innocent persons were arrested and questioned on no other ground than their residence or presence in the area and the presumption that they would have some knowledge of terrorist organisation and activity there. This practice involved the assertion of a general power to arrest and detain any person on the grounds that his identity was not known or that he was suspected of knowing of terrorist activities, a power which, as explained above, was recommended by the Diplock Committee but not provided in the Emergency Provisions Act. To this extent the Army screening operation was of doubtful legality. Of more significance, however, was the fact that it tended to antagonise the population in the Roman Catholic enclaves where it was applied and so ensured a steady flow of recruits for the IRA, especially from among those who had been abused or maltreated in the course of their frequent arrests.

The Royal Ulster Constabulary, on the other hand, appears to have maintained the traditional police approach, except in so far as it was involved through its Special Branch officers in the processing of Army arrests. This police approach was based on the conception that only those persons directly suspected of having committed a specific criminal offence could legitimately be arrested and brought to the police station for questioning, and that only those against whom a specific charge could properly be preferred could be detained in custody.

The difference between these two methods of operation, which may be called the 'military security' and the 'police prosecution' approaches respectively, is crucial to an understanding of the way in which the Emergency Provisions Act was used. It also goes a long way to explain the feeling in Republican areas that 'they' were being treated more harshly than their Loyalist counterparts given the fact that the Army operated principally in Republican areas while the police were largely restricted to Loyalist areas. For these reasons it is worth setting out in some detail the way in which Army screening appears to have worked, even though some aspects of the system could not be fully verified given the highly secretive approach to all 'security' matters.

The Screening System

The new policy of the Army was to establish and maintain as complete a record as was practicable of the population of all militant Republican areas. This covered not only the names and current places of residence of everyone in the area but also a wide range of personal and political information about those suspected of any form of active political or terrorist activity. The basic filing system was maintained at battalion headquarters but the main details were also forwarded to the headquarters of Northern Ireland Command at Lisburn and used as a foundation for the planning of the whole Army security operation.

It was obviously important that the information in this system should be maintained in an up-to-date and accurate form. All Army units were therefore under orders to report any observed changes in the local population and its activities. Meticulous observation and recording of this kind, however, was not regarded as sufficiently accurate or productive. Army units were therefore expected to 'screen' all potential terrorists in their area at frequent intervals.

The primary subjects of this screening process were persons listed on Army files as 'wanted', whose descriptions and photographs would be issued to all soldiers. Soldiers were also expected to take advantage of the local situation to arrest for screening other potential trouble makers whenever the occasion arose, for instance, if they were found outside late at night or otherwise appeared to be acting suspiciously or aggressively. And if for any reason the flow of 'normal' screening arrests from any particular street or district dried up to such an extent that the information on that area was deemed to be no longer adequate for 'operational' purposes, a specific arrest operation might be undertaken with a view to bringing the files up to date. This practice resulted in a number of large-scale arrest operations, like that in the Creggan area in May 1974, in which suspects appeared to have been selected at random and which gave rise to widespread local resentment.

Once arrested the person concerned would be brought to the local screening centre where he would be handed over to the Military Police, given a quick medical examination and then brought before the unit's intelligence specialists. He would then be questioned for anything from five to ten minutes up to several hours both on his own and his family's and friends' movements and on his knowledge, if any, of any recent terrorist incidents or activities in the area. If any useful leads arose in the course of questioning or if any admissions were made, the subject would then be handed over to the police for formal charging, or for further questioning under the seventy-two hour provision referred to above. In any event, the person screened would be given a further medical examination before he was released or handed over to the police. All these stages in the process were meticulously laid down in standing orders from the initial requirement that all persons arrested by Army personnel should be handed over to the Military Police rather than direct to the civilian police, to the detailed forms for medical examination and photographing.

A general picture of the screening process may be obtained from the following account of the questioning of one subject, taken from the depositions on his subsequent committal for a serious criminal offence. The course of events was described in great detail since an allegation of ill-treatment had been made by the accused; this was strenuously denied by the Army officer concerned.

At 16.45 p.m. on 8 June 1973 two young men were 'lifted' in the Markets area of Belfast. There is reason to suppose that both were wanted since a special arrest party was sent out. One of them was formally arrested on the ground that he was suspected 'of being a member of the IRA'. Both were taken to the unit's screening centre at the Grand Central Hotel in Royal Avenue, Belfast. The first suspect was given a routine ten-minute questioning and then the second suspect was brought to the screening room. The officer in charge gave the following account of what happened: 'I proceeded to conduct a routine screening designed to elicit background details concerning (him). I put forward the majority of the questions and occasionally Warrant Officer . . . put a question for the purpose of clearing up any difficulties with respect to local terminology. This initial screening lasted approximately 45 minutes. Initially (he) was asked what role he played in the shooting of Gunner . . . . (He) denied any involvement and continued to deny it when Warrant Officer . . . indicated that he knew (he) was involved. The conversation then moved on to other topics and (he) continued to be unhelpful. At this stage Warrant Officer . . . asked (him) what part he played in the attempted murder of . . . . Much to my surprise the effect of this question was to considerably affect (him). We knew that we had hit on a sensitive area and when he was again asked to describe his involvement he admitted to certain matters. Having achieved this breakthrough (he) was again asked about the shooting of Gunner . . . . (He admitted this and described in some detail the event). . . . Following this he described various other activities and details of matters in which we were interested. . . .' The accused was then medically examined at 19.10 p.m., photographed and handed over to the RMP at 19.15. The RMP handed him over to the RUC at 20.00 p.m. following a further medical examination. At each stage in the process he signed declarations certifying that he was not maltreated by the security forces and that he had no complaints to make against them.

This is clearly an example of a successful screening, but there is no reason to suspect that the procedure outlined was not completely standard or the account of the screening itself untypical.

The Decision of Disposal

The second stage in the military security process under the Emergency Provisions Act began with the handing over of a suspect to the joint Army and RUC Special Branch holding and interrogation centre at Castlereagh in Belfast, or similar centres elsewhere in the province. Here the suspect would again be medically examined and then produced for intermittent interrogation. This could be focussed on the specific incident for which the suspect might be charged, with a view to securing a sufficient admission or confession to ensure his conviction in court proceedings, or else more generally directed to supplementing the flow of information to the security forces on terrorist activities and organisation. It was at this stage that the decision would be made whether the suspect was to be put on trial on specific criminal charges or whether an interim custody order would be sought against him, with a view to putting the case forward for longer term detention without trial. The decision whether or not to prefer criminal charges was apparently made by senior RUC officers, on their assessment of the evidence which had been or might be obtained against the suspect. The decision whether or not to put the case forward for an interim custody order and eventual detention without trial, on the other hand, appears to have been one in which Army intelligence officers played the more important part, in the sense that they were in a position to insist that a particular case was put before the Secretary of State recommending an interim custody order. The grounds on which such recommendations might be made are discussed further in the next chapter.

It is clear from this account that the approach to suspects who were arrested and processed as a result of Army screening was substantially different from that which was adopted in those cases in which the investigation of reported incidents or the arrest of suspects was wholly in the hands of the RUC. In these latter cases the 'police prosecution' rather than the 'military security' approach was dominant in that the whole process of questioning and investigation would be directed towards the ultimate objective of court proceedings rather than the possibility of detention without trial.

46

It seems likely that this difference in approach was deeply rooted in the respective police and Army attitudes to the control of terrorism, and the training to which their officers were subjected. The Army approach would lay most stress on the objective of putting IRA men and to a lesser extent Protestant paramilitants behind bars and would be less concerned with the 'technical' distinctions between conviction in court and detention without trial; the police approach would be centred on the traditional objective of proving a case against the suspect in a criminal court. This is not to say that a number of those arrested by the RUC were not 'processed' in the joint Army/RUC Special Branch interrogation centres and eventually held on interim custody orders with a view to detention or that the traditional police approach was not affected by the existence of emergency conditions and procedures. But there is little doubt that there was a substantial and important difference in the treatment of those suspects who were processed as a result of military and of police activity.

This difference between the Army and police approaches to arrest and questioning was heightened by the fact that the Army operated largely in Catholic and Republican areas, from which independent RUC activity was generally ruled out by local feelings, while the RUC operated with much greater freedom and efficacy in militant Protestant or mixed areas. There is no hard evidence of this differential deployment since it was official policy to emphasise the extent of co-operation between the Army and the RUC and to encourage the belief that both forces operated effectively in all areas. But it is a fact that in mid-1974 about twelve of the total number of eighteen operative Army battalions were stationed in what would be considered to be militant Republican areas, compared with three or four in mainly Protestant areas and two or three primarily concerned in prison guarding or on reserve. An analysis of patrolling patterns, if it had been available, would have made this point even more effectively.

The practical results of this difference in Army and police deployment were twofold. First there was a difference in the nature of the security operation in the two communities. Catholic areas were subjected to what may be termed a communal screening process in which all young people were regarded as potential terrorists and treated accordingly, while in Protestant areas more emphasis was placed on the investigation of specific incidents. Secondly there was a differential flow of suspects into the twin systems of court trial and administrative detention. This helps to explain the huge imbalance in the Republican and Loyalist population of the detention camps which was frequently commented on. In mid-1974, for instance, there were some 500 Republican detainees compared with some 50 Loyalists, though the numbers of cases involving Republicans and Loyalists which came before the courts in the period were roughly equal. This difference in treatment was not a result of deliberate discrimination or partiality on the part of either the Army or the police. It was simply a result of a differential use of Army and police resources which stemmed from the official perception of the nature of the conflict.

Interrogation

There was a similar divergence between the law and practice in interrogation. The Special Powers Act and the Emergency Provisions Act each made specific provision for the detention of suspected persons for the purpose of interrogation. But neither made any alteration in the common law rules relating to the treatment of those persons during the course of their interrogation. In Northern Ireland, as in England, it was unlawful to use any form of physical violence or threats of violence against any person in custody other than what was reasonably necessary to prevent him from escaping or to maintain order in the place of custody. Any policeman or soldier found to have acted without justification in this respect would have been liable both to criminal prosecution and to a civil action for damages. It was also unlawful to prevent prisoners from sleeping or to impose restricted diets other than as a duly authorised punishment under the prison rules. In addition the courts might refuse to admit in evidence any statement deemed to have been made involuntarily as a result of improper pressures. The practice of the Northern

Ireland courts in this respect was somewhat more demanding than in England, in that it had been decided that if an interrogation set-up was oppressive in the sense of making it more likely that those who did not wish to speak would eventually do so, then any resulting statement would not be admitted.[9]

Prior to the introduction of internment in August 1971 there had been no more than occasional allegations of improper conduct on the part of the Royal Ulster Constabulary in the course of questioning, allegations of the kind which are made against most police forces. As soon as the initial internment operation had been completed, however, there was a flood of complaints against the security forces of torture and brutality in the treatment of many of those arrested and in particular those taken to a special interrogation centre established in Holywood Barracks in Belfast. These allegations were given wide publicity and undoubtedly contributed substantially to the re-action against the whole internment operation in the Roman Catholic community. The Committee of Inquiry set up under the chairmanship of Sir Edmund Compton to look into the matter confirmed that 'interrogation in depth' had been undertaken in a number of cases, and that this involved covering suspects' heads with black hoods for long periods, exposing them to continuous and monotonous noise of a kind calculated to make any communication impossible, making them stand against a wall with their legs apart and hands raised against the wall for continuous periods of six or seven hours at a time, and finally depriving them of food and sleep.[10]

These techniques were designed to disorientate those being questioned and so to break down their resistance. They had been developed by the British Army in the course of 'emergency' operations in a number of British colonial territories prior to the granting of independence, and were passed on to RUC Special Branch officers in the course of special training sessions arranged with a view to securing the maximum intelligence results from the internment operation which was being planned. It was never made clear precisely who organised and directed the system of interrogation in depth but it is clear that both Army and RUC officers were involved.[11]

The Compton Committee was not called on to assess the

legality of these techniques, or of the various other practices which it found to have been initiated by the security forces in the course of the initial internment operation. It concluded that many of them constituted 'physical ill-treatment' but not brutality, which in the view of the Committee was 'an inhuman or savage form of cruelty' implying 'a disposition to inflict suffering, coupled with indifference to or pleasure in the victim's pain' (para. 105). This distinction between brutality and ill-treatment was widely criticised but concern over the practices described by the Compton Committee was nonetheless sufficient to induce the government to appoint a further committee under the chairmanship of Lord Parker to consider whether interrogation in depth should be permitted to continue. In the meantime there were continued complaints that persons arrested and interrogated by the Army were being beaten up and otherwise ill-treated.

The Parker Committee was not able to reach agreement on the main issue of policy before it.[12] It was generally agreed that some of the practices described by the Compton report might be unlawful, and that actions for assault, battery and trespass might lie against those responsible, a view which was borne out in subsequent legal proceedings in Northern Ireland, as discussed in detail in chapter 7. But the majority view on the Committee was that the situation demanded tough interrogation techniques and that since nothing unlawful had been or could be authorised under the prevailing military directive the government should take the necessary steps to ensure protection for those taking part in the operation (para. 38). Lord Gardiner, on the other hand, made a minority report arguing that techniques which were in his view clearly unlawful both under domestic and international law could not be justified and were in any event counterproductive. The government eventually adopted Lord Gardiner's view, and announced that no further use of the techniques of interrogation in depth as described by the Compton report would be permitted. This had a marked effect. Though there were continuing complaints in 1973 and 1974 of ill-treatment of suspects during interrogation, notably over the alleged administration of drugs and the use of threats of violence, there can be little doubt that the level of abuse declined sharply. The new procedures for the frequent medical examination of those under interrogation, in particular, appear to have had the result of eliminating much of the direct physical ill-treatment which had been deliberately used or tacitly permitted in 1971 and 1972.

Throughout this initial period the judges in Northern Ireland courts continued to refuse to admit confessions obtained by any intensive method of interrogation in depth on the ground that they had been obtained by oppressive techniques. But this was not to last. The Diplock Committee, which reported in December 1972, took the view that unduly restrictive rules of evidence 'hampered the course of justice in the case of terrorist crimes and compelled the authorities . . . to resort to detention in a significant number of cases which could otherwise have been dealt with both effectively and fairly by trial in a court of law'; it recommended the introduction of a new rule to the effect that only those statements which had been obtained by torture or inhuman treatment as defined in the European Convention on Human Rights should be excluded (paras. 87–91). The legal interpretation of the section in the Emergency Provisions Act which gave effect to this recommendation is discussed in detail in chapter 6. But for operational purposes it meant that while nothing had been done to render lawful any form of physical violence or threats of immediate violence in the course of interrogation, there was now a chance that confessions obtained by illegal methods might nonetheless be admitted in evidence in certain cases. To this extent those in control of interrogation in the security forces were being given conflicting indications of what was and what was not acceptable practice in emergency conditions.

The reasons for this conflict in official attitudes and its results are not hard to explain. There was clearly great pressure on the security forces to produce results. Those involved in the interrogation of suspects knew that they were expected both by the government and by the public at large to maintain a reasonable flow of 'successes' in identifying those responsible for serious terrorist offences. The temptation to use physical violence or threats to induce reluctant suspects to admit to an offence was correspondingly great. In addition those involved in interrogation were members of a small semi-autonomous body of men with a high level of internal group loyalty and a strong sense of purpose. Each one knew that his colleagues would stand by him if any allegations of ill-treatment were seriously pressed against him, and that such allegations could often be discredited as fabrications by terrorists for propaganda purposes. These factors in combination rendered it highly likely both that there would be a certain amount of unlawful conduct in the course of interrogations, and also that none of those responsible would be punished for it. On the other hand, it was clear in the aftermath of the Compton report that politicians would not stand for the kind of gross abuses which had taken place in the initial internment operations. As in other social situations involving conflicting expectations there was a position of minimum strain in which a certain amount of unlawful or improper conduct was accepted as necessary and reasonable by all concerned.

Conclusions

From a broader perspective two conclusions may perhaps be drawn from this account. In the first place it seems clear that the nature of the security operations undertaken in the various periods of the emergency was determined not by the legal provisions prevailing at the time but by the prior commitments of those in control of the operation to certain procedures and methods. This was not just a question of the government balancing the known requirements of the security forces against those of the common law or of international conventions when new legislation was being prepared, though this was clearly done. The fact of the matter is that the law appears only to have imposed certain minor procedural requirements on security policies which had been decided on by the government and the security forces in advance. This is made especially clear by the fact that the Army continued to operate its screening policy in accordance with the proposals which it made to the Diplock Committee, despite the fact that the legislation which eventually emerged from the parliamentary process rendered certain aspects of that policy formally unlawful. Nor is it likely that an open challenge to the legality of the screening policy would have had much effect, given the established tendency of government and parliament to defer to the requirements of the security forces in matters of this kind, as will be seen in chapter 7. In times of armed conflict when the security of the state or internal law and order are under threat, the law is likely to be regarded by those in authority as a weapon rather than a constraint.

It does not follow from this that the decisions of those in authority as to the best use of the weapons at their disposal were always correct. It is difficult to make an accurate judgment as to whether the net effect of the Army screening and interrogation policies in Northern Ireland was beneficial or counterproductive. There is little doubt that they did lead to a flow of much more accurate information on IRA, and to a lesser extent Protestant, paramilitary activities in those areas in which they were implemented. They thus made possible a more comprehensive arrest and detention policy in pursuance of the military security strategy of putting as many terrorists as possible behind bars. But it is much more doubtful whether the adverse effects of the screening policy, when combined with the obvious risk that large numbers of innocent persons would be ill-treated or abused in the course of the arrest and questioning process, was not counterproductive in the sense that it increased the alienation of the civilian population in troubled areas from the security forces, and thus helped to ensure a continuing flow of recruits to terrorist organisations to replace those who were successfully identified and locked up. This aspect of the problem will be discussed in greater detail in the next chapter in relation to internment itself which raises the same issues in a much clearer form.

NOTES AND REFERENCES

1. For the period prior to 1936 see the report of *A Commission of Inquiry appointed to examine the purpose and effect of the Civil Authorities (Special Powers) Acts (Northern Ireland) 1922 and 1933* National Council of Civil Liberties, 1936 (reprinted 1972).
2. *R. v. Governor of Belfast Prison, ex parte O'Hanlon* (1922) 56 I.L.T.R. 170.

3. Volume 17, *sub tit.* Northern Ireland, 1950.
4. *In re McElduff* 12 October 1971.
5. *Kelly v. Faulkner* 11 January 1973.
6. *Detention of Terrorists Order 1973.*
7. *Report of the Commission to consider legal procedures to deal with terrorist activities in Northern Ireland* Cmnd. 5185, London 1972.
8. For further details see 'The Evolution, Disintegration and Possible Reconstruction of the Northern Ireland Constitution' by Claire Palley, *Anglo American Law Review* Vol. 1, 1972, p. 413.
9. *R. v. Flynn & Leonard* 24 May 1972.
10. *Report of the enquiry into allegations against the security forces of physical brutality in Northern Ireland arising out of events on the 9th August, 1971* Cmnd. 4823, London 1971.
11. Some of the techniques are discussed in *Low Intensity Operations* by Frank Kitson, 1973. Brigadier Kitson was directly involved in the planning of Army operations in Northern Ireland.
12. *Report of the Committee of Privy Counsellors appointed to consider authorised procedures for the interrogation of persons suspected of terrorism* Cmnd. 4901, London 1972.

5. INTERNMENT

The ultimate weapon of the state against those who seriously
threaten or attack it from within is temporary or permanent
suppression. In times of war or extreme emergency this may
involve summary execution. In other situations imprisonment,
with or without trial, or banishment may be thought to suffice.
The extent to which the legal system is involved in this process of
eliminating opponents is a matter for political judgment. In some
situations it may be convenient for the government to give an
air of legitimacy to operations of this kind. In others the risk
of an adverse decision at the hands of a system which may not
entirely share the objectives of the government may be too great
to be risked. Whatever means are used, two things are certain:
that those in control are likely to use the legal system in whatever
way they think will best serve their purpose, and that the eventual
outcome is uncertain. General acquiescence in extreme measures
on the part of the organs of the state which must carry them out
and of the population at large cannot be taken for granted.

Internment in Northern Ireland

In Northern Ireland the Unionist government regularly resorted
to internment without trial as a means of dealing with its
military, and to a lesser extent its political, opponents. In the
period up to 1971 internment under the Special Powers Act was
most frequently employed against suspected members or adherents of the IRA, as for instance in the initial period of disorder
in 1921–22, and during the IRA campaigns of 1938–39 and

1956–62. It was also occasionally used on a less systematic basis against leading Republican politicians and activists who were thought likely to throw their support and influence behind subversive activities, as for instance in the case of some leading Republican politicians who were interned for one week during a Royal visit to Northern Ireland in 1951. This use of state power may be seen as legitimate and successful in the sense that it achieved its purpose of preserving the Unionist regime. It may also have been unnecessary in the sense that that purpose could have been better secured by other more democratic means. In either case it certainly alienated large sections of the Roman Catholic population, against which it was exclusively directed, both from the state and its legal system.

On the outbreak of serious disorder in Londonderry and Belfast in August 1969 the Unionist government reacted in the accustomed manner by mobilising its paramilitary police force, the 'B Specials', and interning a number of leading Republicans. This time, however, the operation was not immediately successful and was soon countermanded by the British Home Secretary, James Callaghan, who arrived on the scene in the wake of the British troops which the Unionists had eventually called on to assist them in restoring order. All those who had been detained without trial were released and the government was set on a course of political reform as described in chapter 2. As the renewed IRA campaign built up in the course of 1970 and 1971, however, pressure for the use of the 'ultimate weapon' of internment under the Special Powers Act gradually increased. It was eventually introduced in August 1971 at the behest of the Unionist premier, Brian Faulkner, who had been in control of the successful use of internment during the IRA campaign of 1956–62, despite the opposition of British Army chiefs and of almost all non-Unionist politicians. Their fears that resort to internment in the prevailing state of communal feeling in Roman Catholic areas would make matters worse were fully borne out in the event. The level of violence in the main Roman Catholic enclaves in Belfast and Londonderry increased dramatically, and a number of 'no-go' areas were rapidly established from which the RUC and the British Army were effectively excluded and within which the IRA proceeded to build up its strength and

56

direct its operations. In addition the leaders of the Roman Catholic community as a whole immediately joined forces in calling for a communal rent and rate strike and a general withdrawal from all participation in the state. The strike was widely supported and many leading Roman Catholics withdrew from state agencies.

The principal reason for this united and forceful reaction on the part of the Roman Catholic community was probably the build up of communal solidarity during the course of the previous four or five years of civil rights campaigning and the resulting refusal to accept a return to the old style of Unionist repression. But it was undoubtedly added to by the fact that the list of more than 300 persons arrested and detained included many who were known by the communities in which they lived and worked to have no direct involvement in subversive activities, and by the widespread reports of ill-treatment and torture of those arrested and detained. What appears to have happened is that the main political battle over the decision to use internment was carried out at a high level of generality, without much detailed attention being paid to the question of who was to be interned. The Army did undertake some trial arrest operations in the weeks preceding the initial internment swoop of 9 August 1971, but the list of names appears to have been left to the RUC Special Branch whose knowledge of current IRA organisation and membership was inaccurate and out-of-date. In the words of the Diplock Committee it was 'recognised by those responsible for collecting and collating this kind of information that when internment was re-introduced in August 1971 the scale of the operation led to the arrest and detention of a number of persons against whom suspicion was founded on inadequate and inaccurate information.'[1] Nonetheless the security forces involved in the initial arrest and questioning operation treated all those arrested, many of whom were wholly innocent, as if they were dangerous terrorists.

Once they had embarked on the policy of internment the authorities were reluctant to admit their failure. Though in the months following August 1971 many of those initially arrested were released, many more were arrested and detained: 934 of the 1576 persons arrested under the Special Powers Act between

9 August 1971 and 14 December 1971 had been released by the latter date;[2] on a monthly basis the published figures showed that the proportion of those released to those detained had risen from 33 per cent in August to 75 per cent in November.[3] But the total number detained had crept up to over 500 by mid-November, and to more than 900 by the time of the imposition of direct rule from Westminster in March 1972.

The formal ground for arrest and detention under the Special Powers Act was suspicion that the person concerned was acting, had acted or was about to act 'in a manner prejudicial to the preservation of the peace or maintenance of order' (reg. 11). The final responsibility for the making of an internment order, however, rested with the Minister of Home Affairs who was entitled to order the continued detention of any persons so suspected where it appeared to him to be expedient for securing the preservation of peace and the maintenance of order (reg. 12). The Minister was also personally responsible for ordering the release of internees when it no longer appeared to him to be expedient to keep them in custody. In addition the Act made provision for the appointment of an advisory committee presided over by a senior judicial officer to assist him in reaching decisions on individual cases. In September 1971 Judge Brown was appointed to review the cases of all persons interned, and by December had recommended the release of twenty-five persons out of some hundreds of cases reviewed. The Minister was not bound to accept these recommendations but did in fact do so in all cases. Nonetheless the wholly executive nature of the internment system was clearly maintained and it was generally accepted, as discussed in greater detail in chapter 7, that an internment order could not be effectively challenged in the courts other than on the ground of some procedural irregularity.

The Detention of Terrorists Order

The initial objective of the Westminster government when it imposed direct rule in March 1972 was to phase out the system of internment by a programme of ministerial releases while it sought a political solution by negotiation both with the IRA and with established politicians. In the initial months of direct rule some 500 persons were released by order of the Secretary of State, bringing down the total numbers detained to some 250 persons. When the truce which had been arranged with the IRA broke down, however, it was decided to introduce a new system of detention without trial under which the executive authority of the Minister under the Special Powers Act would be superseded by a judicial determination. Under the new regime detention without trial was portrayed not as a weapon of government against readily identifiable enemies of the state, as it had been by the Unionists, but as a means of dealing with suspected terrorists who could not be dealt with adequately in the ordinary criminal courts, whether by reason of the intimidation of witnesses or the inadmissibility of evidence. This new conception was most clearly expressed in the report of the Diplock Committee: [4]

> We are thus driven inescapably to the conclusion that until the current terrorism by extremist organisations of both factions in Northern Ireland can be eradicated, there will continue to be some dangerous terrorists against whom it will not be possible to obtain convictions by any form of criminal trial which we regard as appropriate to a court of law. . . . We are also driven inescapably to the conclusion that so long as these remain at liberty to operate in Northern Ireland it will not be possible to find witnesses prepared to testify against them in the criminal courts, except those serving in the army or the police, for whom effective protection can be provided. The dilemma is complete. The only hope of restoring the efficiency of criminal courts of law in Northern Ireland to deal with terrorist crimes is by using an extra-judicial process to deprive of their ability to operate in Northern Ireland those terrorists whose activities result in the intimidation of witnesses (para 27).

This new approach was formally sanctioned by a Westminster Order in Council in November 1972, shortly before the Diplock Committee finally made its report. Under the new Detention of Terrorists Order, later incorporated in the Northern Ireland (Emergency Provisions) Act 1973, the cases of all persons detained without trial were to come before an independent judicial Commissioner operating under clearly stated rules, but untrammelled by the rules of evidence applied in ordinary courts of law. In the words of the Diplock Committee, the new system of administrative detention was not to mean 'imprisonment at the arbitrary diktat of the executive government, which to many people was a common connotation of the term "internment"' (para. 28) since the security authorities' case against a suspected terrorist had to be submitted 'to the consideration of some independent and impartial person or tribunal before any final decision to keep him in detention was reached' (para. 32).

There were a number of clearly defined stages in this process.

The first of these was the making of an 'interim custody order' against a person who was 'suspected of having been concerned in the commission or attempted commission of any act of terrorism or in the direction, organisation or training of persons for the purpose of terrorism' (art. 11). Such an order could only be made by the Secretary of State for Northern Ireland or his ministerial deputies (art. 11(2)). It authorised the detention of the person concerned for a period of twenty-eight days, but if the Chief Constable of the RUC made a further order during that period referring the case to a Commissioner for determination the suspect could be held indefinitely until his case was finally determined (art. 11(3)).

The second stage in the procedure was the hearing of the case by a judicially qualified Commissioner appointed by the Secretary of State (arts. 2–4). Before he made a determination that the suspect should be detained further the Commissioner had to be satisfied after enquiring into the case that the suspect had been 'concerned in the commission or attempted commission of any act of terrorism or in the direction, organisation or training of persons for the purpose of terrorism' and also that 'his detention was necessary for the protection of the public' (art. 12). The Commissioner was required to hold a formal hearing in each case in the presence of the suspect and his legal representative, if any, but the hearing was to be in private and the Commissioner could at any time exclude the suspect and his representative in the interests of public security or the safety of any person (arts. 14–17). The suspect was to be supplied with a formal statement of the nature of the terrorist activities alleged against him (art. 13), and the Commissioner had to make a formal record of the proceedings before him (art. 22). Otherwise the Commissioner was entitled to regulate his own procedure (art. 23). Where he was not satisfied that the grounds for detention were established, the Commissioner would order the release of the suspect.

Where a detention order was made by the Commissioner the suspect had a right of appeal to an appeal tribunal comprising at least three legally qualified persons appointed by the Secretary of State (art. 26). The tribunal was required to hold a hearing of the case under similar rules to those for the initial hearing, and had a general discretion to set aside the Commissioner's decision (art. 32).

The next stage in the formal procedure was the requirement that the case of each person detained be reviewed not less than twelve months from the date of the detention order and thereafter at six-monthly intervals (art. 35(1)). The Commissioner was required to hold a review hearing under the same rules as the initial hearing, but was required only to consider the question whether the suspect's continued detention was 'necessary for the protection of the public'; if he was not satisfied about this he had to order the suspect's discharge (art. 32(2)).

The provisions of this new order were clearly much more tightly drafted than for the old system of internment. In each case a charge of what amounted to criminal conduct had to be established against the suspect to the satisfaction of a judicial commissioner at a formal hearing, though without any of the restrictive rules of the common law as to the admissibility of evidence. Nonetheless the essentially executive nature of the detention procedure was maintained by the additional provision that the Secretary of State might at any time direct the release of any person detained either under an interim custody order or a detention order (art. 36). In addition the way in which the system was operated in practice emphasised the 'military security' nature of the detention process in contrast to the normal procedures for judicial prosecution.

An interim custody order was normally made against a suspected terrorist after his arrest and detention for the seventy-two hour period permitted by the Emergency Provisions Act (s.10). Persons arrested under that provision were in most cases conveyed to the joint Army/RUC Special Branch centre at Castlereagh in East Belfast as described in chapter 4. If the questioning of the suspect in conjunction with the evidence already in the hands of the police justified a charge of a criminal offence the suspect would be processed through the Diplock court system, as discussed in chapter 6. If on the other hand it was decided that there was insufficient evidence to justify that, or if it was thought that the evidence available could not be produced in court, the suspect would be considered for an interim custody order.

The formal grounds on which such an order might be made by the ministers of the Northern Ireland Office, as already stated, were that the person was 'suspected of having been concerned in the commission or attempted commission of any act of terrorism or in the direction, organisation or training of persons for the purpose of terrorism'. Soon after the introduction of the new procedure in November 1972, the Secretary of State issued guidelines to the security forces setting out the way in which he would interpret this power so that only those cases which met his requirements would be submitted for his consideration. The substance of these guidelines was that a number of separate traces had to be produced against the suspect indicating his involvement in terrorist activities. Some sources reported that at least six such traces were required. A trace for this purpose might range from direct evidence that the suspect had been involved in a specific terrorist act, as for instance an alleged identification which the witness was not willing to confirm in court, to circumstantial evidence, as for instance the presence of the suspect in the vicinity of the incident, to more tenuous indications of involvement, as for instance association with other 'known' terrorists. Most frequently the principal traces would be the statement of an informer, perhaps supplemented by one or two other more circumstantial and indirect traces to make up the required number. It should be stressed that there was no statutory basis for this system of counting traces.

A further significant aspect of the interim custody order procedure was that no action on the part of the police was necessary either in recommending or commenting on the case made out to the Secretary of State. This meant in practice that Army intelligence officers in Northern Ireland had an independent channel of communication to the Secretary of State, which could be used to ensure the continued detention of any person against whom they could produce the necessary list of traces. There were reports on occasions of disagreement between the Army and the RUC on whether a particular suspect should in fact be recommended for an interim custody order. But in any event it is clear that the existence of this alternative procedure, in which much less attention was directed to the proof of specific criminal acts than in the 'police prosecution' approach, was an integral part of the 'military security' approach to terrorism.

A final important aspect of the interim custody order procedure as it was operated in practice was the fact that in most cases the suspect could be held for a good deal longer than the twenty-eight days specified in the Detention of Terrorists Order. To legalise the extension of custody beyond that period it was necessary for a senior police officer to make a formal reference of the case for determination by a Commissioner, but there is no reason to believe that this was regarded as more than a formality. Many suspects were held on interim custody orders for periods of five or six months or longer pending the hearing of their cases. The practical effect of this was to give to the security forces, and in particular to the Army, the power to arrest and imprison a suspect for around six months without any independent judicial consideration of the case. The fact that in a large proportion of cases the Commissioners ultimately rejected the case made out by the security forces and ordered the release of the suspect is perhaps the best indication of the importance of this power to the 'military security' approach to terrorism in which putting suspected terrorists behind bars was an end in itself.

It is difficult to give a clear statistical base to the picture of the interim custody order procedure which has just been outlined, since the security forces were unwilling to issue regular statistics on the use which they made of their powers in this respect.

No information could be obtained, for instance, on how many cases referred to the Northern Ireland Office for consideration were accepted and how many were rejected until the latter part of 1974 when it was claimed that roughly one in four of recommended interim custody orders were being refused. It seems likely that in earlier periods interim custody orders were much more readily granted. The accompanying table of the number of interim custody orders made is based on a careful analysis of the published figures on Commissioners' hearings, the various forms of release and the net total of persons in custody at given dates. For a number of technical reasons, notably the allocation of releases by the Secretary of State between persons held on interim custody orders and persons against whom a detention order had been made, there may be one or two minor inaccuracies in the figures given in the table, but it is generally correct. For reasons which will become apparent the table is divided into a number of separate periods covering the first and second halves of 1973, the first two months of 1974, the five months from March to July 1974, and the three months from August to October 1974. These periods correspond broadly to developments in the general political attitude to internment on the part of the Westminster government.

The most significant feature of the analysis is the indication it gives of changing levels of military activity in terms of the number of new interim custody orders made in each period. The figures show clearly that the rate of new orders declined from a maximum of just over fifty per month in the first half of 1973 to thirty-five per month in the second half of 1973 and a mere eighteen per month in the first two months of 1974; when the new Labour administration took over in February the rate increased again to thirty-four per month, and then declined on the appointment of the Gardiner Committee in July 1974. Despite these variations, however, the terminal figures of the total numbers of persons held in custody remained remarkably constant from the early part of 1973 up to the end of 1974. Given the commitment of various Secretaries of State to reducing the numbers detained, it is scarcely surprising that the public soon became somewhat sceptical. There is at least some ground for suggesting on these figures that the system of detention

TABLE 5.1: *Figures for the operation of the system of detention of terrorists under the Detention of Terrorists Order 1972 and the Emergency Provisions Act 1973 for selected periods*

Period	No. of new ICOs (estimate)	Average per month	Commissioner's Hearings						Released by Sec. of State	Died and Escaped	Total in custody at start and end of period	
			Initial Hearings		Appeal Hearings		Review Hearings					
			Total	Released	Total	Released	Total	Released			Start	End
January–June 1973	309	51	371	55 (15%)	27	7 (26%)	—	—	8	3	292	528
July–December 1973	208	35	117	41 (35%)	31	5 (16%)	73	26 (36%)	66	4	528	593
January–February 1974	36	18	50	15 (30%)	9	1 (11%)	45	23 (51%)	3	1	593	586
March–July 1974	170	34	134	48 (36%)	61	5 (8%)	184	81 (44%)	32	2	586	589
August–October 1974	53	18	94	34 (36%)	19	5 (26%)	75	28 (37%)	41	[2]*	589	535

* Recaptured

without trial had a momentum of its own, in the sense that the flow of releases tended to be fully offset by the number of new interim custody orders.

Initial Commissioners' Hearings

The procedure for the formal hearing of a suspect's case began with the delivery to the suspect or his legal representative of a list of the terrorist activities which were to be the subject of enquiry. The list usually contained a number of separate allegations derived from the list of traces on the basis of which the initial interim custody order had been made. There was almost invariably an allegation that the suspect was a member of the IRA or other paramilitary organisation at officer level. The remaining items might range from specific allegations that the suspect had been involved in particular terrorist attacks to more general allegations that he had been involved in the organisation and training of terrorists or in the distribution of weapons or explosives, or even on occasions that he had been closely associated with the command structure of a terrorist organisation in a particular area. In some cases there were no specific allegations at all other than of being involved in the organisation and direction of terrorist activities.

In due course, often after further substantial delay, the date for a hearing would be fixed. The suspect was entitled to be represented by a solicitor and counsel of his choice and many were so represented. This legal service was provided entirely at the expense of the Northern Ireland Office so that no application for legal aid was involved. In a standard case in which the hearing took up the best part of a day the joint fee for solicitor and counsel was of the order of £250 – £300, of which about one third went to counsel and the rest to the solicitor. Though groups of lawyers involved in the Commissioners' hearings from time to time threatened to withdraw their services, either because of the unsatisfactory nature of the hearings, or else because of the way in which they had been treated in the detention camp, the legal profession in Northern Ireland in practice continued to cooperate in the system of hearings. This was in part attributable to the duty which individual members of the profession felt they owed to those detained to assist them in any way to regain their freedom; it was also in part attributable to the very substantial remuneration which had been provided, doubtless with a view to encouraging the continued participation of the profession in the system.

The actual hearing of the case took place at the detention camp itself. The sole witnesses for the 'prosecution' were almost invariably members of the security forces. In most cases these gave evidence from behind a curtain, though some regular witnesses whose identity was already fairly well-known did not seek this form of protection. The evidence was normally based on internal Army or RUC reports on the suspect's activities or associations and on statements alleged to have been made by informers. The hearings were frequently adjourned at the request of the police and Army witnesses for the exclusion of the suspect and his representatives on the ground that there would be a risk to the safety of an informer or other person if the evidence were heard in their presence. The full nature of the case against the suspect was thus rarely heard either by the suspect or by his representatives. The only part of the hearing which closely resembled a normal criminal trial was that in which the suspect himself and any witnesses summoned on his behalf were examined and cross-examined under oath.

Informer's Evidence

For practical purposes the principal focus of the initial Commissioners' hearings was the nature and reliability of the evidence of the suspect's involvement in terrorism, and in particular of informer's evidence as reported to the Commissioner by Army and RUC witnesses. This was perhaps inevitable, since if there had been more direct evidence of the suspect's part in specific criminal offences, the case would normally have been tried in the criminal courts.

Much of the cross-examination of the Army and RUC witnesses accordingly concentrated on the twin problems of the quality of the informer's evidence in itself and the reliability of the source. The risks which naturally arise when reliance is place on second and third hand reports are guarded against in ordinary criminal trials by the 'hearsay' or 'best evidence' rule to the effect that in normal circumstances the relevant evidence must be given by the person who actually heard or saw the events in question and not by someone to whom he subsequently related what he heard or saw. The reasons for this are quite straightforward. In the first place, in respect of the quality of the evidence, the precise nature of what is alleged may well become obscured in the process of reporting: a statement that 'X was involved in that bombing', for instance, may cover a wide range of possible circumstances which can only be satisfactorily clarified by further questioning, both as to the nature of the involvement and as to the circumstances in which the witness claims to have seen or heard it. In the second place, in respect of the reliability of the witness, it is desirable that the trial court should itself be enabled to make a judgment as to whether or not or to what extent to accept the truthfulness of the witness by seeing him or her give evidence in person.

In the Commissioners' hearings neither of these requirements could be met. In the case of information which was derived from the confidential telephone system, no-one knew even the identity of the informer and further questioning of any kind was impossible. In the case of known informers who passed on information to the Army or RUC, whether for payment or voluntarily, further probing was possible, but the informer could not be produced nor his identity revealed (at least to the suspect and his legal representatives) in order to protect him against possible retaliation.

The representatives of suspects attempted in some cases to minimise the dangers of unreliable or plainly malicious informer's evidence by questioning the Army and police witnesses as to the precise nature of the evidence and the circumstances in which it was obtained. Some minor forensic victories were won in this process. For a period the Commissioners were persuaded to accept that while simple hearsay evidence might be admitted, 'double hearsay' or 'hearsay upon hearsay', in which the informer was merely passing on something he had heard from another, was altogether too unreliable. But this 'double hearsay' rule was subsequently refined by the Appeal Tribunal to apply only to cases in which the informer could not specify the source of his report. The evidence of some informers was also successfully attacked on the ground that their information had not always turned out to be true. Attempts were also made to discredit alleged informers by arguing that they must either themselves have been involved in the incidents as accomplices, and thus required corroboration, or else that they were not actually present and therefore must be subject to the 'double hearsay' rule. But the opportunities for this kind of cross-examination were strictly limited, given the right of the Army and police witnesses to request the exclusion of the suspect and his representatives in the interests of security. These requests were almost invariably accepted by the Commissioners. This did not in theory prevent the Commissioner himself from probing further in closed session the quality of the evidence and the reliability of the informer. But it was reported by a number of lawyers that further questions put to Army and police witnesses on the resumption of 'open' hearings showed that Commissioners did not normally pursue such a line of questioning.

The Commissioners' Decisions

It will be clear from this brief analysis that in the absence of the traditional common law rules of evidence a heavy responsibility was placed on the Commissioners appointed under the Emergency Provisions Act. Most of these were senior judges or magistrates of a County Court or similar level from Britain or ex-colonial territories who had been brought up in the common law tradition, and who presumably accepted the task out of a sense of duty rather than any liking for the procedures they were operating. The quality of the evidence on which they were called to make their determinations was described as deplorable by one experienced representative at the hearings. The overall result was to make it extremely difficult for the Commissioners to discriminate between important terrorists whose detention might have been productive and suspects whose involvement was peripheral and whose detention helped to convince members of the minority community in particular that the detention system as a whole was both unjust in itself and discriminatory.

Nonetheless the Commissioners, in making their determination as to whether they were satisfied both that the suspect had been involved in terrorist activities and that his detention was necessary for the protection of the public, were careful to emphasise their judicial role: in one case the notes of the Commissioner's decision recorded his statement that 'he had to act judicially and that despite the latitude of procedures allowed by the Act he must in the end see whether the case was clearly established by normal court standards'.[5] On the other hand the general nature of the allegations in some cases made it difficult to maintain this position fully: in a case involving a man alleged to have been an officer of an IRA unit in Belfast in or about October 1970 and to have been concerned in using force against other groups with different political views, and in February 1971 to have had some connection with the murder of one . . ., the Commissioner was recorded as having stated that it was not necessary to be satisfied on the particular form of incident, which did not matter, since he was satisfied that he had some part in it.[6]

In the result the Commissioners appear to have taken a middle line in resolving these conflicting pressures from their judicial background and from the natural desire to make the system of detention effective. Certainly they were far from being mere rubber stamps for executive decisions. After the initial period between January and June 1973 when many of the cases heard concerned those who had been arrested and detained under the old Special Powers Act procedure, the proportion of releases ordered by the Commissioners remained roughly constant at one third. Various interpretations may be put on this fact. An acquittal rate of one in three of all cases in ordinary criminal court proceedings would certainly be regarded as highly abnormal and as a ground for considering whether the prosecuting authorities were properly performing their duties. The high discharge rate in the Commissioners' hearings may perhaps be regarded in the same light, as an indication of the weakness of the case produced against many of the persons against whom an interim custody was made. The fact that the security authorities continued to present cases for the Commissioners' determination with such a high failure rate would on this view be a further indication of the extent to which traditional legal values were eroded by the pursuit of the 'military security' approach.

Appeal Hearings

The formal provision for the hearing of appeals against an initial Commissioner's determination was broadly similar to that for the initial hearing itself. There was accordingly nothing to prevent the appeal tribunal from regarding an appeal as a request for a completely fresh hearing of the case against the appellant. In practice the tribunal adopted a role similar to that of a Court of Criminal Appeal by focussing its attention on formal or substantive defects in the initial hearing and on any fresh evidence which might be produced, and was reluctant to become involved in a simple rehearing of the initial case. This attitude was reflected in the general decline in the proportion of successful appeals shown for the various periods in Table 5.1: in the initial months of the new system the proportion of releases ordered by the appeal tribunal was higher than that of the Commissioners themselves, but after that period the proportion progressively declined to a level of less than one in ten. Given the approach which the tribunal adopted this was perhaps to be expected, as the Commissioners became more familiar with the standards of procedure and evidence which the tribunal developed.

Review Hearings

The matter for determination in a review hearing was essentially different from that in an initial Commissioner's hearing. The

Commissioner was no longer concerned with the terrorist activities which had been alleged against the suspect, which were taken to have been satisfactorily established in the initial hearing, but only with the question of whether continued detention was necessary in the public interest. The main focus of the hearing accordingly shifted from past events to future prospects. In this context the Commissioners generally relied heavily on the views of the security forces. The standard arguments against the release of a suspect were that terrorist activity in the area in which he lived was still at a high level, and that if the suspect were released there was too great a risk that he would again become involved. It was sometimes argued that the suspect's continued commitment to a terrorist organisation within the detention camp itself was further evidence for this. Some persons were formally 'charged' with being camp officers for the purpose of their review hearings: in one case the suspect was formally notified that an allegation of his having been the adjutant of the Provisional IRA in a compound at H.M. Prison, Maze was to be made against him at his review hearing.[7] Where there was evidence that the security forces had 'broken up' the terrorist command structure in an area, there was a greater chance of police or Army witnesses agreeing to the release of a suspect who lived there. The most compelling factor in favour of release, however, was some form of renunciation on the part of the suspect himself of any intention of becoming involved in terrorist activities again.

It will be clear from this brief account that there was little effective role for legal representation in review hearings, except in probing the validity and strength of the views of the Army and police witnesses. Nonetheless the rate of release in review hearings was uniformly high. The figures in Table 5.1 show clearly that the chances of securing release in a review hearing were substantially greater than in an initial hearing, with an overall release rate in the first half of 1974 of not far short of 50 per cent. It is not clear to what extent this reflected a view on the part of the Commissioners that a stronger case had to be made out for continued detention of a particular suspect as time passed or a more general desire on the part of all concerned to keep the numbers detained within 'reasonable' limits. The fact that the rate of release for second and subsequent reviews was only marginally higher than that for first reviews (51 per cent compared with 44 per cent for the first seven months of 1974) suggests that the conception of a suspect having served his 'sentence' was less important than the general view of the security situation which was presented to the Commissioners by the Army and police witnesses. In effect what the Commissioners were called on to determine in these review hearings was the essentially political question whether the general situation in Northern Ireland was such that large or small numbers of those held in detention could safely be released. In performing this difficult task the Commissioners appear to have been guided almost exclusively by the views of the security forces. To this extent the judicial content of review hearings was minimal.

Release by the Secretary of State

The right of the Secretary of State and his ministerial colleagues to intervene at any time in the process of detention and to order the release of particular persons was the clearest demonstration of the non-judicial nature of the system of detention as a whole. At times this power was exercised for openly political motives, as for instance when a number of the most senior Provisional IRA commanders were released in the summer of 1972 as a precondition of the talks between Mr Whitelaw and the Provisional IRA. At other times large numbers of suspects were released with a view to showing the Secretary of State's determination to run down the detention system, or his willingness to make a gesture in that direction, as in the period before Christmas 1973. The power was also used to clear the detention camps of members of the Official IRA when it became clear that their publicly declared cease-fire was genuine and long-lasting.

It is apparent that in many cases of ministerial release the persons concerned would have been equally eligible for release through the system of review hearings, if the Secretary of State had preferred not to intervene. In practice, as can be seen from the figures in Table 5.1, there was a tendency for a high level of ministerial releases to coincide with a lower proportion of releases in review hearings. There was nothing surprising or improper about this. Since likely candidates for release were selected primarily by the security authorities, it was to be expected that in a period when they were required to produce a list of names for release by ministerial direction the proportion of cases dealt with by way of regular review hearings in which the security authorities made no objection to release would decline. But the overlap in jurisdiction in this respect, in conjunction with the abandonment of the notion that the length of detention should be related to the seriousness of the suspect's alleged involvement, further reduced the likelihood of general public understanding or acceptance of the system of Commissioners' hearings as a whole.

Conclusion

This account of the operation of the system of internment under the Detention of Terrorists Order shows clearly how institutional pressures effectively sabotaged the attempt to turn internment from an executive into a judicial system. As in the case of the powers of arrest granted under the Emergency Provisions Act, the Army used the new procedures as a means of putting into effect their own conception of what was necessary for the control of terrorism. The 'military security' approach which it followed was based on the simple idea of putting as many suspected terrorists as possible behind bars. Accordingly the interim custody order procedure, which was intended simply as a short-term holding power, was converted into a means of detaining suspects for periods of up to six or seven months. The requirement of a judicial hearing and the fact that the Commissioners refused to sanction continued detention in more than one third of the cases brought before them made little difference to the Army approach, in the sense that they continued to secure interim custody orders in the kind of case which they must have realised the Commissioners would reject. The power of the security forces effectively to determine the date of release of any person detained by the evidence which they produced at review hearings was a further pointer to the security rather than the judicial nature of the system.

The effect of this general process on public conceptions of the internment system was equally significant. Those who were detained without trial clearly saw themselves and were seen as prisoners of war rather than as persons who had been tried and convicted under a semi-judicial procedure. This conception was particularly strong among the Roman Catholic community both inside and outside the detention camps.

This was partly due to the fact that internment was used almost exclusively against IRA as opposed to Protestant para-military forces. In May 1974, for instance, the number of Protestants detained was approximately 60 out of a total of some 600 detainees; yet at the same time there were some 300 convicted Protestant terrorists in custody out of a total of roughly 900. Thus while Protestants constituted almost one third of those who had been convicted, they constituted only one tenth of those held in detention without trial. The fact that this difference in treatment could be readily explained by differential Army and RUC deployment, as explained in chapter 4, did not lessen the feeling among Roman Catholics that the supposedly judicial nature of the new system of detention was merely a facade to cover the continuation of the old style of executive internment operated by the Unionist regime.

The feeling that those detained under the new procedures were prisoners of war was strengthened by the fact that the internment camps, with their barbed wire perimeters and sentry towers, were obviously modelled on war-time prisoner-of-war camps rather than on ordinary prisons. Conditions inside the camps, under which the prisoners were permitted to organise themselves in a military fashion in each of the huts or cages and in which no work was required, gave further impetus to this attitude, though similar conditions were also imposed on 'special category' prisoners, who had been convicted of terrorist offences. This may have had some bearing on the internal disturbances within the main detention camp at Long Kesh which culminated in the burning down of virtually the whole camp in the autumn of 1974.

On a more general level it is also clear that the new system of detention, like the internment operation of 1971, was a failure in the sense that it made little immediate impact on the IRA campaign, despite the large numbers of supposedly high-ranking IRA commanders who were caught and detained. Since the new system was undoubtedly more selective than the 1971 system in identifying those concerned in one way or another with the continuing IRA campaign, some further explanation must be sought for this. One important factor was the fact that the initial response to the arrest and ill-treatment of so many innocent persons in 1971 was carried over to the new system. Another was perhaps the continuing use of the Army, whose methods were always more forceful and foreign than those of the RUC, in the large-scale arrest and screening process which was an integral part of the new system of detention. A third was perhaps the fact that residents in the main Roman Catholic areas quickly realised that the politicians' assurances that the new system was judicially rather than militarily based were patently false. Finally there was the fact that the scale of the whole security operation meant that substantial numbers of men and youths in almost every street or estate in the main Roman Catholic enclaves were directly affected. This, when combined with the widespread and deeply felt communal antagonism to the whole system, appears to have ensured that sufficient new recruits were continually available to replace those members of the IRA who were successfully identified and detained.

All these factors help to explain why the system of internment which had proved generally effective in 1921–24, in 1938–45 and in 1956–62 was so counterproductive in 1971–74. It is unlikely that this was a result of any major difference in the scale of internment. More than 2000 persons were detained without trial in 1921–24 and the numbers involved in 1956–62 exceeded 600.[8] A more likely explanation is the very different circumstances in which internment was used. In 1921–24 the new state of Northern Ireland was faced with a revolutionary situation and reacted with the utmost vigour. Many of those who opposed the new state were summarily killed by the official and semi-official forces of the Unionists and many more were interned. Equally significant was the fact that the IRA soon became involved in a full-scale civil war in Southern Ireland, which had just gained its independence, and withdrew most of its forces and attention from

Northern Ireland as a result. In 1938–39 and in 1956–62 the situation was again different in that the IRA campaigns were organised and directed from outside Northern Ireland and never gained anything but tacit support from the local Roman Catholic population.[9] The internment of known Republican activists within Northern Ireland as a result appears to have been accepted as a natural if unnecessary and unjustified response on the part of the Unionists. In 1971, on the other hand, the Roman Catholic community had already been united by four years of militant civil rights campaigning and resolutely refused to accept either the principle or the practice of internment without trial. To this extent the effective use of large-scale internment by state authorities may be seen to be dependent in certain circumstances on the acquiescence of the bulk of the local population.

NOTES AND REFERENCES

1. *Report of the Commission to consider legal procedures to deal with terrorist activities in Northern Ireland* Cmnd. 5185, London 1972, para. 32.
2. *Official Report* 828 H.C. Deb., Written Answers, col. 166, 16 December 1971.
3. *Fortnight* No. 32, 26 January 1972.
4. Cmnd. 5185, London 1972.
5. Commissioner Leonard, 15 August 1973.
6. Commissioner Dick, 13 November 1972.
7. *The Times* 31 January 1974.
8. See generally *Internment* by John McGuffin, 1973.
9. See generally *The Secret Army* by Bowyer Bell, 1972.

6. THE COURTS IN EMERGENCY CONDITIONS

Despite the widespread use of internment without trial the courts in Northern Ireland continued to operate more or less normally throughout the period of the emergency. Large numbers of persons alleged to have been involved in rioting or terrorism were dealt with in the ordinary courts on criminal charges. In the initial period of civil rights marches cases were brought against recognised leaders of the civil rights campaign and of the extreme Protestant reaction to it, notably Bernadette Devlin and Ian Paisley, both of whom were jailed. Many others who became involved in confrontations, principally in Roman Catholic areas, were also convicted of riotous or disorderly behaviour. As the scale of the conflict developed many more persons from both communities were charged with more serious offences arising out of bombing and shooting incidents, or with the possession of arms or explosives. At most periods of the developing conflict after the introduction of internment in August 1971 there were substantially greater numbers in custody charged or convicted of criminal offences than detained without trial.

The Unionist and later the Westminster authorities consistently laid great emphasis on the desirability of dealing with unlawful conduct by the ordinary criminal process. In their speeches and press statements they frequently issued encouraging figures on the numbers of persons being charged and sentenced in the courts for terrorist offences, often linked with pleas for greater co-operation from the public in bringing offenders to justice. This tendency became particularly noticeable after the introduction of direct rule from Westminster, when it became official policy to justify, if not to operate, the system of internment without trial on the specific ground that it was made inevitable by the difficulty of dealing with suspects in the courts while the intimidation of witnesses continued. The Diplock Committee was appointed specifically to recommend what amendments of the law of criminal procedure in Northern Ireland were necessary to facilitate the prosecution of terrorists in the courts.[1] And the Secretary of State for Northern Ireland, William Whitelaw, in opening the debate on the second reading of the Northern Ireland (Emergency Provisions) Bill in 1973, emphasised that the government would 'continue to bring suspected persons before the courts wherever possible'.[2]

This official reliance on the criminal courts as the best means of dealing with disorder and terrorism was clearly based on the conception that the legal system would be generally regarded as an impartial arbiter whose decisions would be acceptable in both communities. In practice this was not the case. There were a number of features of the situation which made it extremely unlikely that court decisions would be accepted as just and fair either by militant Protestants or by Roman Catholics in general. The wider implications of this communal lack of confidence in the legal system are explored at greater depth in chapter 7. The purpose of this chapter is to describe the way in which the court system actually operated both before and after the introduction of the new procedures recommended by the Diplock Committee, and in particular to focus attention on those aspects of the system which had a direct bearing on the efficacy of the system as a means of dealing with and discouraging the use of violence.

In the early years of the emergency the main problem was a combination of official and unofficial discrimination in dealing with politically sensitive cases involving Protestant and Roman Catholic defendants. At the official level there was a continuing problem of differential perception on the part of the police and law enforcement officials who tended to regard the main problem as being 'Republican' rioting and terrorism with some element of 'natural' or 'provoked' response from the Protestant extremists. This often resulted in different criteria being applied in dealing with Protestant and Roman Catholic defendants in cases involving objectively similar forms of behaviour. At the unofficial level there was the problem of unjust acquittals, and to a lesser extent convictions, on the part of the predominantly Protestant juries before which all serious cases were tried. As the level of violence increased, additional problems were caused by the intimidation of witnesses and jurors, and a number of more or less technical evidential difficulties in firearms cases. The combined effect of these factors was a cumulative difference in the treatment of Roman Catholic and Protestant defendants which helped to reinforce the traditional distrust of the courts in the minority community.

A series of small research studies carried out in 1972 and 1973 on various aspects of the operation of the judicial system, on which the account which follows is largely based, showed that there was a genuine factual basis to complaints about discrimination in the courts, though the processes which gave rise to the eventual differences were very much more complex than the simple allegations of biased judges and prosecutors implied.[3]

The Pre-Trial Process in Pre-Diplock Trials

The first element in the cumulative process of differentiation was a degree of difference in approach by the police to Protestant and Roman Catholic suspects. In riot cases there was a tendency for charges of riot to be preferred against Roman Catholics and less serious charges of disorderly behaviour to be preferred against Protestants. This was particularly noticeably in cases where there were confrontations between Protestant and Roman Catholic rioters. The police tended in such cases to face the Roman Catholic crowd and turn their backs to the Protestant crowd and to make most of their arrests from among the Roman Catholics. This was understandable in the sense that the main focus of Roman Catholic attacks was the policemen themselves, while the Protestants would usually direct their missiles against the Roman Catholics; but it clearly served to convince the minority community that the RUC was a sectarian force. There was also a tendency to regard the possession of arms as a more serious offence on the part of Roman Catholics than Protestants. In the period before 1972 this might perhaps have been justified in the sense that most of the shooting originated from the Roman Catholic side, but the tendency was continued into 1972 and 1973 at a time when there was an increasing number of armed attacks by Protestants on Roman Catholics.

In so far as the actual choice of charges was concerned, any discrimination on the part of the police should have been eliminated after the establishment in 1972 of the new independent and impartial prosecuting authority, the office of the Director of Public Prosecutions. But in practice the new system had less immediate impact than was intended. In the first place the new system did not take over full control of the selection of charges in less serious cases of firearms possession and rioting until well into 1973. And secondly the Director's staff of lawyers was entirely dependent on police reports of cases, so that the primary decision on whether or not to prefer charges and what kind of evidence to collect and report was made by the police. The Director did have power to order the collection of further evidence, but the initiative in this respect clearly rested with the police.

A number of examples may be given of the way in which these pre-trial processes were operated, both in the selection of charges and in the related question of release on bail or remand in custody.

In the early part of 1972 teams of student observers were sent into magistrates courts in Belfast and other parts of the province to report on the performance of the courts in 'political' and 'ordinary' criminal cases,[4] with particular reference to the frequent allegations of discrimination in the granting of bail. In all 114 relevant bail/custody decisions were observed: of these 74 were classified as 'political' cases, mainly firearms and explosives charges and a few cases of assault and wounding, and 40 as 'ordinary' crimes, covering property offences and other miscellaneous crimes. As might be expected most of the remands in custody were made in the 'political' cases: bail was granted in 16 per cent of these, compared with 78 per cent of the cases in which the nature of the charges were revealed and classified as 'non-political'.

Within these two main categories, however, there was a substantial difference in the treatment of Roman Catholic and

Protestant defendants, as shown in Table 6.1. The situation was complicated by the fact that a number of defendants charged with 'political' crimes refused to recognise the court and were thus procedurally barred from applying for bail. It may be assumed that these defendants were Roman Catholics in view of the established IRA tradition of refusing to recognise the legitimacy of Northern Ireland courts. But even if these cases are excluded, there was still a substantial difference in treatment between Roman Catholics and Protestants: only one in five (21 per cent) of the remaining Roman Catholics charged with 'political' crimes were granted bail compared with almost half (46 per cent) of the Protestants. There was no such difference in treatment in respect of 'non-political' crimes.

TABLE 6.1: *The number and proportion of Protestant and Roman Catholic defendants granted and refused bail in a sample of cases in the magistrates courts in 1972*

Type of offence and religion	Bail granted		Bail refused		Total	
	No.	%	No.	%	No.	%
'Political' offences						
Protestant	6	46	7	54	13	100
Roman Catholic	6	21	22	79	28	100
Refused to recognise court	—	—	31	100	31	100
Religion unknown	—	—	2	100	2	100
Subtotal	12	16	62	84	74	100
'Non-political' offences						
Protestant	8	47	9	53	17	100
Roman Catholic	6	50	6	50	12	100
Refused to recognise court	—	—	7	100	7	100
Religion unknown	2	50	2	50	4	100
Subtotal	16	40	24	60	40	100

One reason for this difference in treatment was the fact that the Roman Catholics in the sample cases had generally been charged with more serious offences, though as will be seen this did not always mean that their actual behaviour was more serious. Another factor was the attitude of the police, who played an important part in the decision on bail. It was customary for magistrates to ask police witnesses for their view on the granting or refusal of bail in particular cases. In the survey the question of bail was openly discussed in fifty-five of the cases, and in almost all of these the police witnesses expressed a view. There was again a substantial difference in the approach to Protestant and Roman Catholic defendants: police witnesses objected to bail in 95 per cent of the 'political' cases against Roman Catholics, compared with only 60 per cent of the 'political' cases against Protestants. Some of this difference may have been due to the more serious nature of the charges against the Roman Catholics in the sample, but the case reports also showed that the police witnesses often argued that Roman Catholics were in general less likely than Protestants to answer bail, since they might well evade the jurisdiction of the court by crossing the border, or alternatively that it might be more difficult and dangerous for the security forces to re-arrest a defendant in a Roman Catholic area than in a Protestant area. There was some justification for these views. The security forces at the time frequently came under attack in Roman Catholic areas, and figures produced in reply to a parliamentary question showed that in the space of a year sixty-nine persons had absconded while on bail. Furthermore the authorities and the courts in the Republic consistently refused to extradite any person wanted for a 'political' crime in the North. Nonetheless there was a clear element of sectarian bias in the thinking of the police on this issue.

The magistrates in the sample cases went some way to correct this bias by granting bail to four of the nineteen Roman Catholics whose release was opposed by the police witnesses, and by refusing bail to two Protestant defendants in whose cases no police objection was raised. Yet there were a number of cases in which the final decision appeared unduly favourable to Protestant defendants. In one instance a Protestant charged with possession of a firearm and ammunition was granted bail on the grounds, which the magistrate accepted without question, that there was no political motive in the case. Any person who was refused bail by a magistrate had a right of appeal to a High Court judge, and in a number of such cases bail was granted. In addition the Director of Public Prosecutions had been entrusted with the duty of advising the courts on the exercise of their powers to remand on bail or in custody. But neither of these safeguards appears to have succeeded in eleminating the overall difference in treatment. A subsequent survey of 159 Protestants and 158 Roman Catholics whose cases were put down for trial at the Belfast City Commission in the first half of 1973 showed that bail had been granted to twice as many Protestants (59 per cent) as Roman Catholics (27 per cent).[5] Though as before part of the difference may have been due to the more serious nature of the charges against the Roman Catholics, there is little doubt that differences in police perception of Protestant and Roman Catholic defendants played a major role in this respect.

A similar form of conscious or unconscious discrimination could be detected in the selection of charges against Protestant and Roman Catholic defendants, both for the summary trial of less serious cases and for jury trials. In the sample of cases covered in the magistrates courts survey in 1972 this was particularly apparent in respect of riotous and disorderly behaviour. At this time a conviction for riotous behaviour carried an automatic sentence of six months imprisonment, while one for disorderly behaviour did not. Eleven cases of riotous behaviour were covered in the sample, in all of which the accused was a Roman Catholic; twenty-one cases of disorderly behaviour were covered, in which eight of the defendants were identified as Protestants and eleven as Roman Catholic. A more detailed consideration of the circumstances of these latter cases revealed at least three cases against Protestant defendants in which a charge of riotous behaviour would appear to have been warranted. In one of these the defendant was in a crowd of youths throwing stones at the Army from behind a UDA barricade; the magistrate commented that there was nothing political about the case, though it was a serious offence, and imposed a fine. In another a 19-year-old Protestant girl was charged with disorderly behaviour after being arrested from a crowd which was stoning troops. In the third case a Protestant who was alleged to have been encouraging a crowd to engage in hostilities with a rival crowd was likewise charged with disorderly behaviour. In some of the cases the magistrates themselves expressed their concern over the selection of the charge: in two cases of riotous behaviour against Roman Catholics the magistrates remarked that they would have preferred to convict the accused on charges of common assault. It seemed clear that in cases such as these there had been an element of bias on the part of the police in the selection of charges.

After the establishment of the office of the Director of Public Prosecutions in 1972, as already stated, any bias on the part of the police should have been eliminated by the independent consideration of all charges. But for practical purposes the police were still in a position to influence the final choice through the reports which they submitted on each case. What happened in practice was roughly as follows. The defendant was arrested and questioned, as described in chapter 4. Then if a decision to prefer formal charges was made by the police officers concerned, he would be remanded in custody on a holding charge pending further police investigations, a process which might take up several months. On the completion of these investigations, the police officer responsible for the case would submit his report and a recommendation to his superiors of the precise offences to be charged. These senior officers would then examine the file and might either approve the recommended charges or add additional or alternative recommendations of their own. It was only at this stage that the file was lodged with the Director of Public Prosecutions who made the final decision on the charges to be preferred and the mode of trial. This may account for the fact that an element of difference in treatment of Protestant and Roman Catholic defendants continued into 1973. This was most apparent in the selection of firearms charges.[6]

There were three broad categories of firearms charges under the Firearms Act (Northern Ireland) 1969: the most serious were possession with intent to endanger life (s.14), possession with intent to resist arrest (s.15), and possession with intent to commit a crime (s.16), for which the maximum sentences ranged from ten to fourteen years' imprisonment; a second group of charges comprised the carrying of firearms in a public place (s.17) and possession in suspicious circumstances (s.19A), for which the maximum sentences were five years; the least serious charges were possession of firearms or ammunition without a certificate (s.1), for which the maximum sentence was three years' imprisonment.

What appears to have happened is that while there was some measure of equal treatment of Protestant and Roman Catholic suspects in the choice of the more serious charges there was a tendency for the least serious charges to be omitted in cases involving Roman Catholics, while they were more frequently included in cases involving Protestants. Official figures for cases actually tried at the Belfast City Commission between January and June 1973 showed that while there was only one case against a Protestant defendant in which only a charge of possession without a certificate was preferred, such charges were included in four out of ten cases against defendants identified as Protestants (38 per cent) compared with less than three in ten cases against Roman Catholics (28 per cent), as shown in Table 6.2.[7] A more detailed analysis, on a somewhat different basis, of these cases along with a number of others set down for trial at the Commission but adjourned for trial at the Belfast Recorder's Court or in a subsequent Commission, indicated that the main

TABLE 6.2: *The selection of charges against defendants identified as Protestant and Roman Catholic in firearms cases tried at the Belfast City Commission, January – June 1973*

	Religion of defendants*			
Nature of charges	Protestant		Roman Catholic	
	No.	%	No.	%
'No certificate' charges only	1	1	—	—
'No certificate' charges combined with more serious charges	37	38	27	28
More serious charges only	60	61	70	72
Total persons charged	98	100	97	100

For details of the statistical base of this table see Appendix A.

difference arose in those cases where arms were found in suspects' cars or in their physical possession, rather than as a result of searches of houses or otherwise. As shown in Table 6.3 the least serious 'no certificate' charges constituted more than a third of the total counts against defendants identified as Protestants in such cases, compared with less than one in seven of the total counts against those identified as Roman Catholics.[8] Part of this difference may have been due to the fact that Roman Catholics tended to be found in possession of rifles, whereas Protestants

TABLE 6.3: *The total number of counts preferred against defendants identified as Protestant and Roman Catholic in firearms cases set down for trial at the Belfast City Commission January – June 1973, analysed according to the circumstances in which the arms were found*

Nature of charge	Search of car or person				Search of house				Other circumstances			
	Prot.		R.C.		Prot.		R.C.		Prot.		R.C.	
	No.	%	No.	%	No.	%	No.	%	No.	%	No.	%
No certificate (s.1(a) and 1(b))	60	36	14	13	32	47	26	32	8	8	2	2
In public place/in suspicious circumstances (ss.17 and 19A)	61	37	51	49	25	37	28	36	41	40	43	46
To endanger life/to resist arrest/to commit crime (ss.14–16)	44	27	40	38	11	16	26	32	54	52	48	52
Total counts	165	100	105	100	68	100	80	100	103	100	93	100

For details of the statistical base of this table see Appendix A.

were more often found with handguns, as discussed below, and in any event the prosecuting authorities probably devoted most of their attention to the choice of the more serious charges. But the small difference in approach in this respect, when combined with the difference in approach by the juries before which the cases were tried, contributed to the overall difference in the outcome of firearms cases which was so readily observable in this period.

Conviction and Sentence in Pre-Diplock Cases

One of the first reactions on the part of the authorities to the increasing incidence of rioting in 1969 and 1970 was to introduce a mandatory prison sentence for cases of rioting. Under the terms of the Criminal Justice (Temporary Provisions) Act (Northern Ireland) 1970 magistrates were required to impose a six-month prison sentence on all persons convicted of riotous or disorderly behaviour. This measure immediately caused problems, since it was found that a number of cases of domestic dispute in which charges of disorderly behaviour were regularly preferred were falling under the terms of the new statute, and the law was soon amended to exclude cases of disorderly behaviour. Nonetheless the operation of the mandatory sentence continued to give rise to difficulties and complaint. Some magistrates were clearly reluctant to impose prison sentences in some of the cases which were brought before them: in one case covered in the 1972 sample survey the magistrate remarked that the compulsory sentence was too high, but had to be imposed; in another the magistrate remarked that it was with the greatest reluctance that he imposed the mandatory six months' imprisonment. Members of the public were also reported to have been openly dissatisfied with the mandatory sentences imposed in certain cases.[9] Similar difficulties arose in certain firearms cases which also fell under the terms of the new statute: in one case a Protestant youth who had been taken to the police by his father when he was found with a single round of ammunition had to be given a six-month sentence; in another a Roman Catholic convicted of possession of an empty shotgun cartridge likewise had to be sentenced to six months' imprisonment. Cases such as these clearly served to decrease the level of public confidence of both communities in the administration of justice in the magistrates courts.

The magistrates were also faced with a problem of a rather different kind in dealing with riot cases. In a typical case, as reported by the observers in the 1972 survey, there were two entirely separate stories as to the circumstances in which the defendant was arrested, that of the soldiers or police and that of the defendant. There was a direct conflict of this kind in all but one of the cases in the sample. In the majority of cases the magistrates in the end accepted the version given by the security forces, as might be expected. The courts were clearly under pressure from the security forces and the public at large to convict those brought before them in order to deter others from becoming involved in disturbances. But in a number of cases it was difficult to accept that the charges had been proved beyond reasonable doubt, as for instance in the following examples:

Case A   There was rioting in Derry between 2.00 pm and 7.00 pm. At 4.00 pm, a youth in white shoes was observed in the riot through binoculars from an Army observation post. At 7.00 pm, the defendant, who was wearing white shoes, was seen by an Army patrol and arrested, because the patrol had been informed that one of the rioters was wearing white shoes. The defendant denied the charge and claimed that he was elsewhere at the time. He was found guilty.

Case B   A corporal in a patrol in the Falls Road in Belfast stopped the defendant and asked his identity. Shortly after, according to Army witnesses, a crowd gathered and began to throw stones at the patrol. Army witnesses claimed that the defendant was at the front of the crowd, but no arrest was made at the time. Later the patrol came across the defendant again, going away from the scene of the trouble, and arrested him for riotous behaviour. The defendant claimed it was a case of mistaken identity, and that when he was arrested he had been standing in a doorway with his girlfriend; if he had been rioting, he claimed, he would have run away when the patrol approached him. The magistrate agreed that it was a problem of identification but found the defendant guilty.

Case C   A soldier on top of some flats picked out three youths from a crowd which was rioting. The youths then moved off and the soldier lost sight of them. A minute later he claimed that he saw one of the youths again, and that he was able to recognise him because he was wearing a denim jacket and trousers. The defendant was arrested by a patrol on instructions from the soldier. The defendant claimed that it was a case of mistaken identity, and that denim jackets and trousers were common items of clothing in the area. The defendant was found guilty.

Cases such as these show clearly the problems faced by magistrates. Riot cases were politically and emotionally significant, and people in the area would soon know if any injustice had been done. In such cases the sense of injustice would have been exacerbated by the behaviour in court of some Army witnesses who, according to observers' reports, made no attempt to conceal their pleasure at obtaining a conviction. Yet little attention appears to have been paid by the authorities to ensuring that only the clearest cases were brought before the courts. The desire to keep up the number of arrests and convictions appeared in some cases to have taken precedence over the maintenance of public confidence in the courts.

The problem in the higher courts where conviction and acquittal were in the hands of a jury was rather different. The outcome of criminal trials on indictment was dependent on a complex interaction between the judge, the jury, the prosecuting authorities and the defendant. But it soon became clear that the largely Protestant juries were causing an unacceptable level of difference in treatment between Protestant and Roman Catholic defendants. In cases where Roman Catholics were involved the judges were able to prevent the juries from convicting in doubtful cases by using their power to direct an acquittal. But in cases involving Protestant defendants there was nothing the judges could do to prevent a jury acquittal on all or the most serious charges. A full account of the processes involved and the results which it produced in individual cases is beyond the scope of this chapter, but the broad outline of what was happening can be explained.

The qualifications for jury service in Northern Ireland were based on the ownership of property and ensured that the vast majority of those on the jury list were Protestants. For each Commission some three hundred names would be selected from the list in such a way that those eligible would come up for service in rotation. From this initial panel up to a third or a quarter might be excused by special application to the court on the ground of special personal or business circumstances. The jury of twelve persons for each individual case was then selected from those remaining on the panel by drawing cards at random from a box in the court room and in the presence of the judge and the legal representatives of both sides. The prosecution was entitled to 'stand by' any number of jurors; the defence might challenge up to twelve jurors for each defendant without giving any reason, and might object to other jurors for good cause.

In practice these rights of stand by and challenge were used in such a way as to secure a predominantly Protestant jury in cases against both Roman Catholic and Protestant defendants. In cases against Roman Catholics the prosecution used its rights of stand by to exclude any Roman Catholic jurors who lived in troubled areas. In theory, the ground for this was that such persons were especially open to intimidation and should not be permitted to serve in the interests of their own safety, but it was also understood that Roman Catholic jurors might tend to favour Roman Catholic defendants. In cases against Protestant defendants, on the other hand, the defence would be equally anxious to exclude all Roman Catholic jurors, since they would be less inclined than Protestant jurors to be lenient, and would thus challenge all those on the jury panel who appeared to be Roman Catholics either from their names or addresses or any other information available to the solicitors in the case. Those concerned in the administration of the jury system in Belfast indicated that the defence right to challenge without cause was more frequently exercised than the prosecution right to stand by, but that challenges for cause were extremely rare: in one case it was reported that there had been forty-four challenges and twenty-three stand bys. The net result was that most Belfast juries were almost exclusively Protestant, though juries in assize trials in other parts of the province were generally more representative.

The risk in these circumstances that juries would discriminate in favour of Protestant defendants and against Roman Catholic defendants was obvious, and as more and more Protestants began to come before the courts for serious offences in the course of 1972 and 1973 there was increasing concern over this aspect of the judicial system. In the debate on the second reading of the Emergency Provisions (Northern Ireland) Bill the Attorney-General referred to a number of cases at a recent assize at Armagh in which the verdicts in cases involving Loyalists appeared to his informants to be contrary to the evidence: in one instance a man found in a car with a gun was acquitted of unlawful possession of firearms; in another three men who were seen to throw a gun from a car being pursued by an Army patrol were also acquitted; in a third case, arising out of the hijacking of a lorry, there was again an acquittal though the goods had been found in a UDA club and the documents were in the handwriting of the accused; in the fourth the leader of a UDA unit who had been identified as taking part in an armed robbery was also acquitted.[10] Following the Attorney-General's speech there were a number of similar allegations arising out of the acquittal of leading Protestant paramilitants in Belfast.

The results of the official survey of all cases heard at the Belfast City Commission in the first six months of 1973 provided further evidence of this kind of bias.[11] The analysis of the outcome of all charges preferred against all defendants, as set out in Table 6.4, showed a substantial difference in the proportion

TABLE 6.4: *The outcome of all charges preferred against Protestant and Roman Catholic defendants, and those whose religion could not be identified, in cases heard at the Belfast City Commission, January – June 1973*

Outcome of each charge	Protestant		Roman Catholic		Unknown	
	No.	%	No.	%	No.	%
Plea of guilty	215	47	65	15	17	45
Convicted by jury	45	10	185	44	4	11
Charge withdrawn by DPP	84	18	91	21	3	8
Not guilty by direction of judge	40	9	58	14	2	5
Acquitted by jury	71	16	25	6	12	32
Charges disposed of	455	100	424	100	38	100
Charges not disposed of	12		73		3	

For details of the statistical base of this table see Appendix A.

of jury acquittals in respect of defendants identified as Protestant (16 per cent) and Roman Catholic (6 per cent). By using their power to direct acquittals the judges in these cases went some way to restore the balance, but by a combination of pleading guilty to less serious charges and relying on a jury acquittal for more serious charges a number of Protestant defendants clearly secured a more favourable outcome than was open to Roman

Catholic defendants. It was particularly noticeable from the official figures that the jury acquittal rate on charges against those identified as Protestant was higher than the average on the more serious charges of attempted murder (37 per cent), other offences against the person (47 per cent), and the more serious arms charges (s.17: 29 per cent; s.19A: 22 per cent).[12] This pattern also had an effect on the level of sentences imposed on Protestant and Roman Catholic defendants, since the judges naturally determined the length of sentence in accordance with the charges for which convictions were returned. An analysis of all sentences imposed in respect of each type of firearms charge, as set out in Table 6.5, showed clearly that there was a clear pattern in the average sentences imposed on each type of charge, with a higher tariff for more serious charges.[13] The fact that slightly higher average sentences were imposed on defendants identified as Catholics in respect of some of the charges, though this may have been justified by differences in the type of firearms involved as discussed below, further contributed to the feeling among the minority that the courts were biased in favour of Protestants.

TABLE 6.5: *Average sentences for firearms charges imposed on defendants identified as Protestant and Roman Catholic in cases tried at the Belfast City Commission, January – June 1973*

Nature of charge	Protestants	Roman Catholics
No certificate for firearms (s.1(1)(a))	9 months	12 months
No certificate for ammunition (s.1(1)(b))	11 months	11 months
Possession in suspicious circumstances (s.19A)	2.3 years	3.3 years
Possession in public place (s.17)	2.3 years	3.4 years
Possession with criminal intent (s.16)	4.2 years	6.3 years
Possession with intent to endanger life (s.14)	6.4 years	6.8 years

For details of the statistical base of this table see Appendix A.

The authorities were also concerned at this period with the number of cases in which defendants were acquitted in the courts on what were regarded as merely technical defects in the case again them. In a number of cases the judges held that confessions by the defendant were inadmissible on the ground that they had not been voluntarily given. And in some firearms cases they directed an acquittal because of the rule that where guns or explosives were found in a house or vehicle in which there were a number of occupants the prosecution had to establish that one or other of them was legally in possession. According to the Attorney-General there had been almost one hundred cases in which prosecutions had to be abandoned for one or other of these reasons.[14] The response of the security forces to cases of this kind, as to perverse jury acquittals, was frequently to rearrest the defendant at the door of the court under the terms of the Special Powers Act or the Detention of Terrorists Order. The Attorney-General revealed that such action had been taken in thirty cases between March 1972 and May 1973, though he stressed that defendants would not be rearrested merely on the basis of the evidence which had been rejected by the courts without other evidence of involvement in terrorist activities.[15] Whatever the truth of this latter claim, this practice clearly added to the general distrust of the courts on the part of the Roman Catholic community, as discussed in chapter 7. It was also a very clear indication of the dissatisfaction on the part of the authorities both with the system of jury trial and with the rules of evidence applied by the judges, and may help to explain some of the recommendations eventually adopted by the Diplock Committee.

The Diplock Committee

In discussing the obstacles to dealing with terrorist crimes in the ordinary criminal courts the Diplock Committee identified three major problems: first, the intimidation by terrorist organisations of witnesses who might have been able to give evidence for the prosecution (para. 7); secondly, the danger of perverse acquittals of Loyalist terrorists by predominantly Protestant juries, whether as a result of intimidation or of partisan attitudes (paras. 36–37); and, thirdly, the existence of technical rules of law on the proof of possession and the admissibility of confessions which greatly enhanced the difficulty of obtaining convictions of guilty men

94

(para. 59).[16] The Committee concluded that the first of these problems made the maintenance of some form of administrative detention unavoidable, given the provision in the European Convention for the Protection of Human Rights and Fundamental Freedoms that the cross-examination of witnesses by or on behalf of the accused person was an indispensable element in a criminal trial (art. 6). But it also concluded that the remaining problems could be largely circumvented by the suspension of jury trial, the introduction of amended rules of evidence for the trial of terrorist offences, and the imposition of more stringent controls on the granting of bail, which the Committee considered was being granted more freely and indiscriminately than the emergency situation demanded.

All these recommendations were based almost exclusively on the views of the prosecuting authorities and the security forces. No evidence was received either from the Northern Ireland judges or those practising in the courts, or from the public and their representatives. This in itself was perhaps the best indication of the extent to which the Diplock Committee saw its task as one of remedying certain loopholes and inadequacies in the security system rather than of improving the standards of justice being achieved in the courts. There was no discussion in the Committee's report of the inherent contradiction in seeking to encourage the use of the courts and public confidence in them while at the same time maintaining a system of extra-judicial detention which struck at the very root of public conceptions of justice according to law.

Nonetheless the substance of the Diplock Committee's recommendations was eventually enacted by the Westminster Parliament in the Northern Ireland (Emergency Provisions) Act, 1973. The basis of the Act in so far as the criminal courts were concerned was the creation of a new category of 'scheduled' offences covering broadly all those crimes regularly committed by terrorists and their supporters. The various provisions of the new statute for the suspension of jury trial, the amendment of the rules of evidence and the hearing of applications for bail applied only in respect of these scheduled offences, notably murder and other serious offences against the person, almost all firearms and explosives offences, arson, robbery, aggravated

95

burglary, intimidation and some other related crimes. The trial of all scheduled offences was to be centralised in Belfast. The purpose of the rest of this chapter is to consider in some detail the effect of these various provisions both on the internal operations of the court system and more generally on public attitudes to the administration of justice, in the light of an analysis of all the cases dealt with under the new procedures from September 1973 to March 1974.[17]

The suspension of jury trial
The justification for considering trial by jury to be an important part of a system of criminal trial is the protection which it should afford against oppression or unreasonable conduct on the part of the police, the prosecuting authorities or the judiciary. Studies in various common law jurisdictions of the way in which the jury system operates in practice have generally confirmed that this is something which juries do in fact achieve.[18] In a divided community such as Northern Ireland, however, the value of this communal safeguard against officialdom is likely to decrease as intercommunal passions and loyalties are aroused. The reality of this danger has already been demonstrated. The main question is thus whether the suspension of jury trial for scheduled offences in Northern Ireland under the Emergency Provisions Act (s.2) did in fact succeed in eliminating sectarian bias in jury verdicts without sacrificing the safeguards which the jury system ideally provides in a settled community.

The answer to the first part of this question on the evidence of those cases tried in Diplock courts in the first seven months of their operation is quite clear. The figures in Table 6.6 show that any bias on the part of juries in favour of Protestant defendants was entirely eliminated: treating each trial as a single unit for the purpose of analysis, regardless of the number of defendants and charges, the overall acquittal rate for cases against Protestant defendants was 5 per cent for the full period of the survey, compared with an acquittal rate of 13 per cent for cases against Roman Catholic defendants. Virtually all these acquittals were in respect of the possession of firearms. The higher acquittal rate for Roman Catholic defendants may then be explained by the fact that more Roman Catholics than

Protestants were able to establish to the satisfaction of the judge that they were acting under duress or did not know of the presence of the firearms. The acquittal rate for Roman Catholics was in fact substantially the same as that in cases tried before the introduction of Diplock courts, in which there had been a high level of directed acquittals. In addition a substantial number of Roman Catholic defendants continued to refuse to recognise the court, in accordance with IRA tradition, and thus lessened whatever chance of acquittal they might have had. In this sense the introduction of non-jury trials made little difference in cases against Roman Catholic defendants. In respect of Protestant

TABLE 6.6: *The results of trials for scheduled offences heard in Diplock courts at the Belfast City Commission from September 1973 to March 1974*

Outcome	Sept.–Dec. 1973				Jan.–March 1974				Total			
	Prot.		R.C.		Prot.		R.C.		Prot.		R.C.	
	No.	%	No.	%	No.	%	No.	%	No.	%	No.	%
Plea of guilty	36	72	11	27	44	71	20	31	80	71	31	30
Plea of guilty to lesser charge	4	8	4	10	5	8	6	9	9	8	10	10
Found guilty	4	8	14	35	7	11	30	47	11	10	44	42
Found guilty on lesser charge	2	4	3	7	4	6	2	3	6	5	5	5
Found not guilty	4	8	7	17	2	3	6	9	6	5	13	12
Not proceeded with	—	—	1	2	—	—	—	—	—	—	1	1
Total cases	50	100	40	100	62	100	64	100	112	100	104	100

defendants on the other hand there was a substantial shift in practice towards the making of a guilty plea in respect of all charges preferred, in place of the previous tendency to plead guilty only to less serious charges and to hope for a lenient verdict from the jury, as indicated in Table 6.4. It would appear that the legal representatives of Protestant defendants were now advising their clients that there was more to be gained under the new system of Diplock trials from pleading guilty and relying on the judge's leniency than from seeking an acquittal on the more serious charges. To this extent the suspension of jury trial was clearly successful in removing an important source of difference in the treatment of Protestant and Roman Catholic defendants.

On the other hand the figures in Table 6.6 suggest that the suspension of jury trial did remove a potentially valuable safeguard in the sense that the danger of 'automatic' convictions by the judges appeared to increase as time passed. The rate of acquittal declined sharply from a figure of 17 per cent in respect of cases against Roman Catholics and 8 per cent in respect of cases against Protestants in the first four months of the new system of Diplock trials, to a rate of 9 per cent in cases against Roman Catholics and 3 per cent in cases against Protestants in the second period of the survey. These figures indicate that there was a measure of acclimatisation on the part of the judges sitting in Diplock trials and an increasing readiness to accept the evidence of the police and security forces in preference to that of the defence.

This pattern of declining acquittal rates did not result from any lack of attention on the part of the judges in Diplock courts to the difference between the role of judge and jury in criminal trials. It was clear from the reports of observers in the Diplock courts that all the judges were anxious to maintain the various procedural rules which had been developed in the common law jury system. In the first place they were careful to preserve the right of the defence to make a submission of 'no case to answer' at the close of the prosecution case, and in a number of instances went through the explicit verbal process of asking themselves as judges whether they were satisfied that there was sufficient evidence for them to permit themselves to consider the merits of the case in their capacity as juries. They were also careful to maintain the rule that the prosecution case had to be proved beyond reasonable doubt. In some cases the judge made explicit his view that while he himself had no doubt about the guilt of the accused, his feeling that a reasonable juryman might have had a doubt had induced him to enter an acquittal. While some aspects of this careful distinction between the role of judge and jury appeared to observers to have become an exercise in mental gymnastics, the principle which the judges adopted did emphasise the continuity between the old and the new systems of trial.

The removal of the lay jury, however, did have a considerable impact on the conduct of cases in Diplock courts, in that many aspects of the trials were carried on primarily on the basis of documentary evidence and depositions rather than the verbal evidence of witnesses. This was in part due to the special circumstances prevailing in Northern Ireland, in which the available evidence was often limited to confessions or admissions and to a consideration of the circumstances in which they were made, due to the widespread fear and intimidation of witnesses. But the elimination of the jury did reduce the scope for the traditional skills of advocacy and cross-examination, and led to more direct discussion between counsel and judges on the basis of the written statements. There was also an increase in the extent to which the judges themselves sought to take a direct part in the elucidation of the truth by questioning witnesses and counsel. The overall effect was to replace the more theatrical aspects of the traditional jury trial as a contest between two sides with a more sober search for truth, and to emphasise the extent to which the trial process had become a 'closed-shop' in the hands of a small group of professional lawyers.

Changes in the rules of evidence

Three substantial changes in the rules of evidence for the trial of scheduled offences were made by the Emergency Provisions Act: first the shifting of the burden of proof in certain firearms cases (s.7); secondly the relaxation of the common law rules on the admissibility of confessions (s.6); and thirdly the provision for the admission of signed statements in certain circumstances in which it was impractical to produce a witness in court (s.5).

The provision for the shifting of the burden of proof in firearms cases was specifically designed to remove the difficulty created by the decision in an earlier case in which a gun had been found in a bedroom in which three brothers slept: all three had been convicted by a jury of unlawful possession of the gun, but the conviction had been quashed on appeal on the ground that there was insufficient evidence to show that any one of them was actually in legal possession of the weapon. To remedy this, and the related problem posed in cases in which guns were discarded by unidentifiable members of a group of persons when confronted by the security forces, the Diplock Committee recommended that the burden of proof should be shifted onto the accused in cases where firearms were found in his place of residence or wherever he happened to be when they were discovered (paras. 68–72). The Emergency Provisions Act accordingly provided that where a person was charged with the possession of firearms, ammunition or explosives and it was proved that he had been present in or habitually used the premises or vehicles while the articles were there, the court might take this as sufficient to establish his possession of them unless he showed that he did not know they were there or if he did that he had no control over them (s.7).

This provision appears to have worked satisfactorily, in the sense that persons accused of the possession of firearms or explosives were forced into giving some account of their knowledge of the matter. This meant that the cases were decided primarily on the credibility of their evidence rather than on legal technicalities. Nonetheless the courts continued to apply the common law rule that despite the section the onus was still on the prosecution to prove guilt, and in a number of cases accepted that the occupier of a house in which arms or explosives had been found either did not know of their presence or had been forced into keeping them against his will. This defence was accepted in nine of the twenty-four cases of arms finds in houses brought against Roman Catholic defendants and in three of the fifteen cases brought against Protestant defendants in the first seven months of the new procedure. But where arms were found in the defendants' vehicle or in their direct control, there were many fewer acquittals: in the same period only four of the twenty-seven cases against Roman Catholic defendants and only two of the twenty cases against Protestant defendants resulted in an acquittal on all charges. In cases in both categories, however, where one of several persons charged with joint possession agreed to accept responsibility, the rest were normally discharged. To this extent the new provision did not entirely deal with the problems raised by the Diplock Committee, in the sense that in a number of the cases it was clear that one of the accused had agreed to 'take the rap' in order to secure the release of his colleagues.

The second major alteration in the rules of evidence for the trial of scheduled offences concerned the admissibility of confessions. Given the widespread intimidation of civilian witnesses and the justifiable fear of reprisals, confessions and admissions obtained from suspects in the course of interrogation soon became the major ground of conviction in the criminal courts. Yet, as has been described, there had been a substantial number of cases in which the judges had ruled that such confessions and admissions were inadmissible on the ground that they had not been voluntarily given. The Diplock Committee concluded that the current rules on admissibility were 'hampering the course of justice in the case of terrorist crimes and compelling the authorities . . . to resort to detention in a significant number of cases which could otherwise have been dealt with both effectively and fairly by trial in a court of law' (para. 87). It recommended that the restrictions imposed by the Northern Ireland version of the Judges' Rules on the questioning of suspects after their arrest should be suspended, and that the rule developed by the Northern Ireland High Court that any interrogation set-up which was oppressive in the sense that it made it 'more likely that those who did not wish to speak would eventually do so' would render any resulting statement inadmissible should be suspended for the duration of the current emergency (paras. 81–84).

In making these recommendations the Diplock Committee was careful to reject any implication that it condoned the methods of interrogation in depth involving prolonged wall-standing, hooding and deprivation of food and sleep which had been used in 1971 and subsequently prohibited (para. 86). The Committee sought to draw a line between what was acceptable and unacceptable in interrogation techniques by falling back on the provisions of the European Convention on Human Rights which prohibited absolutely any form of torture or inhuman or degrading treatment. Accordingly it recommended that only those statements which had been obtained by torture or inhuman or degrading treatment, or the threat of such treatment, should be inadmissible (paras. 89–91). This recommendation was duly given effect in the Emergency Provisions Act which provided that in the trial of scheduled offences the court might accept in evidence any relevant statement made by the accused unless 'prima facie evidence was adduced that the accused was subjected to torture or to inhuman or degrading treatment in order to induce him to make the statement'; in such cases the court was to exclude

101

the statement, or if it had been admitted already continue the trial disregarding it or direct a new trial before a differently constituted court, unless it was satisfied by the prosecution that the statement had not been so obtained (s.6). It should be noted that this formulation was wider than that recommended by the Diplock Committee in that no reference was made to threats of torture or inhuman or degrading treatment.

This provision was clearly effective in the sense that statements which would previously have been excluded by the judges were admitted in evidence in Diplock trials. The judges interpreted the section in such a way as to retain for themselves the ultimate discretion to admit or reject statements which had been obtained by methods of interrogation short of torture or inhuman or degrading treatment but which would previously have been inadmissible:

> In considering the admissibility of the alleged confession I am of the opinion that notwithstanding section 6 of the Northern Ireland (Emergency Provisions) Act 1973 the court has a discretion to exclude as inadmissible confessions obtained or which might have been obtained by oppressive conduct or in oppressive circumstances or obtained by threats or hope of advantage. Conduct and circumstances which are relevant to the voluntary nature of a confession in the trial of a non-scheduled offence may be invoked in my opinion in the trial of a scheduled offence as a basis for inviting a Court, in the exercise of its discretion, to exclude it on the ground of unfairness.[19]

But up to the end of 1974 there was only one case in which a confession statement was ruled inadmissible under the terms of the Act. In the case already cited the judge went on to admit a statement which had allegedly been obtained following a severe beating of the accused by the security forces, threats of handing him over to the UDA and subsequent prolonged questioning in which, though his father was present, any objection on his part was brushed aside: in the words of the judge 'one of the matters which the court could well take into account in exercising its discretion was the existence of section 6 . . . and its object'; questioning in his view 'must be persistent and robust'. In another case in which allegations of the production of a jar of acid and other threats of ill-treatment had been made and in which the judge himself found that the accused had been poked in the stomach, the judge likewise admitted a confession on the ground that the defendant was well able to stand up to such treatment; he added that unless there was more than mere threats, unless there was a real fear of inhuman or degrading treatment, he would admit a confession under the provision. In other cases confessions were admitted in spite of evidence that offers of lenient treatment had been made to the accused and that juveniles had been persistently questioned without a determined effort being made to ensure that a parent or other representative of the juvenile's interests was present in accordance with the instructions which had been issued to the police.

To this extent the judges clearly accepted and gave effect to the intention of the new provision, and gave some measure of judicial approval to robust and persistent interrogation. On the other hand the number and seriousness of complaints of ill-treatment in the course of interrogation declined sharply in the course of 1973 and 1974. In the cases tried from September 1973 to March 1974 at the Belfast City Commission there was only one instance in which there was any independent evidence to support allegations of torture: in that case, which had been carried over from a previous Commission and was thus tried before a jury, medical evidence of recent burning was produced to support the allegation of torture by lighted matches and the accused was acquitted of those charges in respect of which he made the confession. All the other cases in which allegations of ill-treatment were raised concerned persons suspected of being connected with the IRA, and in all of them the judge explicitly rejected the most serious of the allegations on the ground either that they had not been proved or that they had been grossly exaggerated.

It is difficult in view of the conflict of evidence to reach any firm conclusion on the effect of the new legal rules on standards of interrogation. In so far as there was any improvement in the conduct of those who carried out the interrogation of suspected terrorists it appears to have resulted from internal administrative directives rather than judicial control. In addition the relaxation of the rules on admissibility created a new danger that the security forces would take advantage of the provisions of the new Act in cases involving known IRA suspects, in the knowledge that any allegations of ill-treatment of IRA suspects would be likely to be held to have been fabricated for propaganda purposes or exaggerated to such an extent that the confessions obtained would in the end be admitted. The effect of this strategy, however, in so far as it was adopted, was clearly counterproductive in terms of public confidence in the courts. Trials in which allegations of ill-treatment were made always received wide publicity in the local press, and the ambiguous position in which the judges were placed under the new Act rendered them even more open to criticism. There was widespread concern and comment, for instance, over the peculiar situation which arose in the Tohill case, in which the judge admitted a disputed confession of involvement in an attack on a military patrol on the part of one of the accused, but rejected its validity in the face of a strongly supported alibi. In more general terms the attempt to facilitate the conviction of suspects in the courts by removing one of the most important safeguards of the common law clearly demonstrated the inherent contradiction of seeking to combine a tough security approach to the control of terrorism with increased reliance on public confidence in the decisions of the criminal courts.

The final and least controversial recommendation of the Diplock Committee on the rules of evidence was that certain written statements should be admissible in evidence when the person who had made them had been killed, or had left the jurisdiction or could not otherwise be produced. All of these were eventualities which might well arise in Northern Ireland. Yet such statements would have been inadmissible under the ordinary hearsay rule of the common law. The Committee gave its general support to the principle behind the hearsay rule on the ground that 'to estimate the probative value of a statement made by a person who is not called as a witness at the trial it is necessary to know who and what manner of man he was, to whom and in what circumstances the statement was made, what opportunities the maker had of seeing or hearing accurately each of the incidents that his statement records' (para. 100). As these were the very details which in Northern Ireland had often to be kept secret in order to protect witnesses from retaliation, the Committee concluded that no major alteration of the hearsay rule could solve the special problem of dealing with terrorist crimes in the courts, and that any minor relaxation should be strictly limited to cases in which a signed statement was made to the police or other responsible authority.

This limited recommendation was duly enacted in the Emergency Provisions Act, which provided that signed statements made by any person in the presence of a constable might be admitted in evidence if the person who made it was dead or unable to attend by reason of his bodily or mental condition, was outside Northern Ireland, or could not be found (s.5). The provision was relied on once or twice in cases where a prospective witness was shown to be medically unfit to give evidence, but did not prove to be of any great significance. The prosecuting authorities did not seek to make use of it to introduce in evidence statements made to the police by witnesses who refused to appear by reason of fear or intimidation, on the ground that to do so would be too great a departure from the normal procedures of a criminal trial. The policy of the Director of Public Prosecutions was that it would have been wrong to bring in evidence which could not be subjected to cross-examination except in special circumstances. Whether or not this was a correct interpretation of the purpose of the provision, it is clear that the prevailing values of the legal profession made it unlikely that it would be used in a bold or extensive manner. As in other situations of a similar kind, the legal profession preferred to maintain its established practices and to leave to others the less attractive aspects of the security system.

Diplock trials: *the pre-trial process*
The remaining aspects of the system of Diplock trials are best considered in the more general context of the operation of the system as a whole. The account which follows is based on a detailed analysis of all the cases heard by Diplock courts at the Belfast City Commission from September 1973 to March 1974: this covered the vast majority of scheduled offences tried during that period, the remainder having been transferred for trial at the Belfast Recorder's Court for administrative convenience. In contrast to the overall analysis of all separate charges against all

105

defendants on which the account of the pre-Diplock jury trials was based, each trial was treated as a separate unit, and classified into one of seven exclusive categories, in accordance with the broad nature of the incidents out of which the trial arose. These were as follows:

  (i) firearms finds in houses;
  (ii) firearms finds on the defendant's person, in his car or otherwise in his admitted personal control;
  (iii) attacks by shooting or explosives on members of the security forces by Roman Catholics, and similar sectarian attacks by Protestants on Roman Catholics;
  (iv) the planting, preparation or transport of car-bombs, gas cylinder bombs, duffle bag bombs, and other explosive devices directed primarily against property;
  (v) armed robbery, including cases involving imitation firearms;
  (vi) other terrorist offences, including kidnapping, arson, intimidation, accidental shootings and other forms of personal attack.

The object of this classification was to permit an analysis of what might be thought of as a layman's view of the various terrorist crimes rather than a formal legal view of the particular charges preferred. In addition, for ease of analysis, each trial was considered as a separate unit, regardless of the number of individual defendants and counts, taking the most serious finding of guilt and the most severe sentence as the best indication of the outcome of the trial. There are some obvious drawbacks to this form of analysis, but it seems likely on balance to give the best overall picture of the operation of the system. The number of cases in each category against Protestants, Roman Catholics and members of the security forces in the period of the survey is set out in Table 6.7.

The first stage in the process under the new procedure was the decision on bail. The Diplock Committee considered that in the period immediately before its report bail was being granted by magistrates in Northern Ireland 'much more freely and indiscriminately', even for the most serious offences, than would have been the case in England; in the opinion of the Committee this was unacceptable both in that it increased the risk of the

TABLE 6.7: *The nature of the offences dealt with in Diplock trials against Protestants, Roman Catholics and members of the security forces, September 1973 – March 1974*

	Firearms in houses	Firearms on person or in car	Murderous attacks on security forces or civilians	Bomb attacks on property	Robbery	Other	Total
Cases against Protestants	35	20	7	7	33	10	112
Cases against Roman Catholics	24	27	9	26	12	6	104
Cases against security forces	—	—	1	—	—	3	4

intimidation of witnesses and of further terrorist outrages, and also in that it had 'a serious effect on the morale of the troops to see a known terrorist, whom they had arrested, perhaps at the risk of their own lives, the week before, walking the streets a free man in the area from which he had been operating' (para. 54). It accordingly recommended that for those charged with terrorist offences remands in custody should be mandatory except on application to a High Court judge, and that any such application should be refused except where the judge was satisfied both that there was no risk of the defendant failing to answer his bail, interfering with witnesses or committing further offences, and also that exceptional hardship would be caused to him by further remand in custody, or else that he had been in custody already for 90 days without being committed or tried (para. 55).

In the Emergency Provisions Act the general principle of the Diplock Committee's recommendation that only the High Court should have power to grant bail was adopted, but the suggested restrictions in relation to exceptional hardship and the 90-day rule were not enacted, thus giving the High Court a general discretion in the exercise of its original and appellate jurisdiction subject to statutory guidelines to the effect that the judge was to be satisfied that the applicant would comply with any conditions imposed on him, would not interfere with witnesses and would not commit any further offences (s.3).

These new provisions in respect of bail did not give rise to any major problems and were not subjected to any substantial criticism. An analysis of decisions on the granting of bail in respect of those persons tried at the Belfast City Commission between September 1973 and March 1974, comparing those decisions which were made before the introduction of the new procedures with those which were made under the new procedures, suggests that the kind of inequality in the treatment of Protestant and Roman Catholic defendants described above was largely eliminated. Though an exact comparison was not possible since any person could apply to the High Court for bail

TABLE 6.8: *The results of applications for bail by persons charged with scheduled offences whose cases were tried at the Belfast City Commission from September 1973 to March 1974, showing the difference between applications dealt with primarily under the old and the new procedures*

| Type of offence | Religion | Old procedure | | | New procedure | | |
		Persons No.	Bailed No.	%	Persons No.	Bailed No.	%
Firearms finds in houses	Protestant	9	5	33	33	18	55
	Roman Cath.	25	9	36	26	12	46
Firearms on person or in car	Protestant	29	19	66	28	23	82
	Roman Cath.	15	4	27	38	17	45
Murderous attacks on security forces or civilians	Protestant	5	—	—	15	—	—
	Roman Cath.	20	7	35	10	—	—
Bomb attacks on property	Protestant	5	2	40	13	1	8
	Roman Cath.	13	—	—	33	—	—
Robbery	Protestant	19	16	84	62	12	19
	Roman Cath.	5	2	40	23	4	17
	Unknown	1	—	—	2	—	—
Other	Protestant	7	3	43	19	8	42
	Roman Cath.	15	5	33	13	3	23
	Unknown	2	1	50	2	—	—
	Soldiers	2	2	100	4	2	50
TOTAL	Protestant	73	43	59	169	62	37
	Roman Cath.	93	27	29	145	36	25
	Other	5	5	60	8	2	25

at any time, and since in some cases some of the bail decisions were made before and some after the introduction of the new procedures, an ad hoc allocation of the decisions on the basis of the date of final remand for trial or the release on bail, as shown in Table 6.8, showed that while there was little change in the proportions of Roman Catholic defendants who received bail, there was a marked decline in the comparable figures for Protestant defendants under the old and the new procedures. The remaining difference between the two communities, primarily in cases involving the possession of firearms, was probably attributable to the less 'serious' nature of the firearms on the Protestant side and a number of cases involving off-duty members of the Ulster Defence Regiment in unofficial possession of firearms. This aspect of the problem is discussed further below. On a more general level it may be noted that the relatively high level of releases on bail for scheduled offences showed clearly that the courts continued to approach the problem from an individual judicial point of view rather than the blanket security viewpoint implicit in the recommendations of the Diplock Committee. Nonetheless the judges appeared to have been remarkably successful in reducing the number of defendants released on bail who subsequently failed to appear for trial. In the period covered by the survey a greater number of persons failed to appear for trial following an escape from lawful custody, particularly in the case of juveniles remanded to approved schools, than as a result of absconding while on bail.

The procedure for the selection of charges was not affected by the introduction of the new system of Diplock trials. But in the period covered by the survey the Director of Public Prosecutions appeared to be ensuring a degree of equality of treatment of Protestant and Roman Catholic defendants which had sometimes been lacking in the selection of firearms charges in the earlier period. In cases classified as 'firearms finds in houses' and 'firearms on person or in car' alike the full range of relevant charges was preferred from possession without a certificate to possession in suspicious circumstances or in a public place. In cases classified as 'murderous attacks on security forces or civilians' in which the firearms had actually been used or were apparently about to be used the least serious charges of possession without a certificate were normally omitted. The main difficulty in these cases was the selection of the more serious charges, and in particular whether to prefer a charge of attempted murder for which a life sentence might be imposed or one of possession of firearms with intent to endanger life for which the maximum sentence was fourteen years. There was a tendency in cases of this kind to infer a greater readiness on the part of IRA members to use guns found in their possession for offensive purposes than in the case of Protestant defendants. In one case involving three men found with a loaded revolver and balaclava helmets in a stolen car late at night, the Director issued the following instruction to the police: 'Withdraw the holding charges under s.14 [possession with intent to endanger life] and prefer charges under s.19A [possession in suspicious circumstances] and s.17 [possession in a public place]; while the presence of a working firearm together with balaclava helmets arouses the gravest suspicion judges have repeatedly declined to convict on this grave offence unless there is evidence of intent very much stronger than this.' In a case against a youth found with several rifles and loaded magazines in his bedroom and alleged to have admitted being in the IRA, however, the judge held that though there was no evidence that the youth himself would use the rifles to endanger life there was ample evidence from their past use in murderous attacks to support a charge that he had them with intent that others should so use them. This difference in approach to cases involving IRA members was part of a wider difference in perception on the part of the law enforcement system as a whole and will be discussed in greater detail in relation to sentencing.

Diplock trials: conviction and sentence
The removal of the element of bias in jury decisions, as discussed above, was the principal factor in securing a greater degree of equality in the outcome of trials involving Protestants and Roman Catholics in Diplock courts. The remaining differences in the processing of cases against Protestant and Roman Catholic defendants turned largely on the attitude of the defendants themselves. Following the suspension of jury trial, as is shown by the figures in Table 6.6, the vast majority of Protestant defendants entered pleas of guilty to some or all of the charges preferred against them. Those Roman Catholic defendants who were members or adherents of the IRA, however, continued to refuse to recognise the courts on the ground that any state institution which derived from the partition of Ireland lacked legitimacy. In such cases a formal plea of not guilty would be

entered on the defendant's behalf and the trial proceeded without his participation. Defendants who refused to recognise the court were acquitted in a handful of cases, but in the vast majority the refusal to recognise was taken as an admission of membership of the IRA and as equivalent to a plea of guilty. In pactical terms the main significance of refusal to recognise lay in the level of sentence which could be expected as a result.

The most satisfactory way of explaining the sentencing process in terrorist offences, both in jury and Diplock trials, is to focus on the six main categories of terrorist crime which have already been isolated rather than on the sentences imposed for particular legal offences, and to attempt to establish both the 'norm' and the various aggravating and mitigating factors which appear to have influenced the judges in settling on individual sentences within each broad category. For this purpose the most severe sentence imposed on any of the defendants was taken as the fairest indication of the overall outcome of the case. In the sections which follow the sentences imposed in cases heard from September 1973 to March 1974 in each of the main categories will be discussed in turn, with a view both to elucidating the approach adopted by the courts and to assessing the validity of the widespread complaints of continuing discrimination on the part of the judges against Roman Catholic defendants.

(i) Firearms finds in houses

There was a wide variation in the sentences imposed in cases in which firearms had been found as a result of house searches by the security forces, ranging from suspended and other non-custodial sentences to a maximum in one case of eight years' imprisonment. The factors which appear to have influenced the outcome most strongly were the nature of the arms and explosives found and the presence or absence of evidence that the defendants were involved in any terrorist organisation. For those found with a handgun or a shotgun and only a small amount of ammunition a sentence of one or two years was normally imposed. Where there were exceptional circumstances justifying a claim that the weapon was kept entirely with a view to self-defence, as for instance evidence of previous attacks or threats of attack, this might be reduced to a non-custodial sentence.

111

Non-custodial sentences were also normally imposed in cases where part-time or full-time members of local security forces, and in particular the Ulster Defence Regiment, were found to have weapons at home without authorisation. On the other hand, possession of a rifle normally led to a sentence of three or four years, and where what might colloquially be regarded as an 'arsenal' of several rifles, handguns and assorted ammunition was found four or five years' imprisonment would be imposed. In these respects there was no immediately apparent difference in the treatment of Protestant and Roman Catholic defendants other than the fact that rifles were more frequently found in Roman Catholic houses. This resulted in a generally higher level of sentencing against Roman Catholic defendants both on charges of possession in suspicious circumstances and of possession with intent to endanger life.

The second important factor which contributed to the generally higher level of sentences against Roman Catholic defendants was their alleged association with or membership of the IRA. This was frequently a ground for the selection of the most serious charge of possession with intent to endanger life, as noted above. Membership of or association with Protestant paramilitary associations, notably the UDA, on the other hand, was not generally regarded as an aggravating factor, and membership of the Ulster Defence Regiment was often taken as a ground for the mitigation of sentence. This difference in approach to the IRA and Protestant paramilitary organisations, in conjunction with the differences in the weapons normally found in their possession, appeared to account fully for any differences in sentences imposed on Protestant and Roman Catholic defendants in this category.

(ii) Firearms finds on person or in car
There was a similar variation in the sentences imposed in respect of firearms found in the defendant's personal control, whether as a result of a street or vehicle search or otherwise. In some cases the judges took a lenient view, often in the light of the youth of those involved: in one case a band of Roman Catholic youths in a rural area who had been found in a stolen car with a shotgun and who admitted possession of a cache of other firearms stated

112

to be for the protection of their housing estate were all given suspended sentences by a Protestant judge; in another a Protestant youth who had been found with a pistol, which he claimed was 'for the good of Ulster', as a result of a street search in Londonderry was also given a suspended sentence by a Roman Catholic judge. In all the Diplock trials in this category non-custodial sentences were imposed in four out of twenty-three cases against Roman Catholic defendants compared with six out of eighteen cases against Protestant defendants. On the other hand, where there was evidence of membership of the IRA and the weapon was a rifle, sentences of four or five years, and where there was a conviction of possession with intent to endanger life, sentences of six or seven years were regularly imposed. It was again noticeable that Protestant defendants were more often found with handguns and Roman Catholic defendants with rifles.

(iii) Murderous attacks on the security forces and civilians
Armed attacks on the Army or the police by members of the IRA and armed sectarian attacks by Protestants on Roman Catholic civilians represented the most serious category of offences and generally attracted the most severe sentences. Where the victim was killed and a conviction of murder was entered a life sentence was necessarily imposed. There were two cases of this kind against Roman Catholic defendants and one against a Protestant defendant in the period covered in the survey. In two cases against Protestant defendants, however, charges of murder were rejected and convictions for manslaughter and impeding arrest were entered, with sentences of five years and eight years respectively; in the first of these there was some evidence that the accused was mentally retarded and in the second the judge held that there was insufficient evidence to show that the defendant had actually fired the fatal shots, though he had clearly been directly involved in mounting the attack.

Where the attacks did not cause death the sentences imposed varied from three to fifteen years. Fifteen years was the normal sentence where a conviction of attempted murder was entered and was imposed in three cases against Roman Catholic defendants and one case against Protestant defendants. In one case against Catholic defendants a sentence of eight years was imposed and in one against Protestant defendants a sentence of twelve years. The differences in these sentences appear to have resulted from the judges' assessments of the degree of active involvement by the defendants in the attack. Where there was not a conviction of attempted murder the normal sentence was between five and seven years; this was imposed in five cases involving Roman Catholic defendants and one case involving Protestant defendants. The three cases in which the relatively lenient sentences of three years were imposed on Roman Catholic defendants arose out of bombing attacks in which it was accepted by the court that serious injury to the security forces was not intended.

(iv) Bomb attacks against property
Sentences in cases involving substantial bombs normally varied between five and fifteen years. The variations again appeared to depend on the judges' assessments of the size and seriousness of the bomb itself and the degree of involvement on the part of the particular defendants. The least severe sentence against a Protestant defendant was of borstal training for a rather ineffectual attempt to set off a gas cylinder bomb in a Roman Catholic chapel; the least severe sentence against a Roman Catholic defendant was of two years imposed on a young man found with a bomb in his car in Londonderry. The most severe sentence in a case involving Protestant defendants was of twelve years for a bomb attack on a Roman Catholic public house in Belfast; the most severe sentences against Roman Catholic defendants were imposed in the Coleraine car-bombs case, as a result of which a number of civilians were killed, and in which a life sentence on a charge of murder was imposed, and in a case against a man found to have been directly responsible for at least three substantial bomb attacks on businesses in Belfast in which a fifteen year sentence was imposed. Between these extremes there was no evidence of any systematic difference in approach to defendants from the two communities, though one or two individual sentences appeared to be somewhat out of line. Omitting two cases in which indeterminate sentences of life imprisonment and borstal training were imposed, there was a remarkable similarity in the average sentence imposed in cases

114

involving Protestant defendants (8 years) and Roman Catholic defendants (7.7 years).

(v) General conclusions on sentencing
No useful comparative analysis could be carried out on the sentences imposed in the remaining types of scheduled offences other than robbery. The normal sentence in cases of robbery involving defendants who were deemed to be fully responsible lay between five and eight years, but there was a substantial number of cases in which lesser sentences were imposed, usually because of the youth of those convicted or the intrinsic 'triviality' of the incident, as for instance where young boys went into small shops with imitation guns. But two further general comments may be made on sentencing practice across the whole range of scheduled offences.

In the first place it is clear that there was substantial variation in the sentences imposed in all the categories dealt with, regardless of the religion of the defendants. It might be argued that in a situation in which selective and unfair comparisons were frequently made for propaganda purposes, such variation was undesirable in itself. But there would be equally serious objections to any system in which mandatory or uniform sentences had to be imposed for particular offences, given the huge range of variation in the circumstances of individual cases and in the degree of involvement by individual defendants. The experience of mandatory sentences for rioting in the period between 1969 and 1972, as discussed above, showed clearly that flat rate sentences for all offences of a particular kind gave rise to as much if not more discontent among the friends and relatives of many of those affected as allegations of bias in discretionary sentencing. There was no simple solution other than to encourage a greater awareness on the part of individual judges and magistrates of the dangers of differences in approach and perception, but in the last resort to leave the level of sentence to the discretion of the judge or magistrate concerned, in the light of all the various aggravating and mitigating circumstances.

On the other hand it is equally clear that the approach which was adopted by the judges to cases involving members of the IRA and the various Protestant paramilitary organisations, and to the type of weapons which they habitually used, contributed to the feeling among members of the minority community that Roman Catholic defendants were being unfairly treated. From the point of view of the judges membership of the IRA and the use of rifles and bombs against the security forces represented a more serious attack on the institutions of the state and society than the reaction which this attack provoked from the Protestant paramilitary organisations. Some judges openly expressed the view that the IRA was in itself a more seriously illegal association, given that its principal object was the destruction of the state of Northern Ireland, than the UDA and other Protestant associations which had not been formally proscribed and which had been formed mainly in response to IRA activity. From the point of view of the minority community, however, this approach was regarded as biased and discriminatory. In their view, the fact that the IRA was illegal and the UDA was not, was merely a result of an unjustifiable decision on the part of those in authority. And the difference in their habitual weapons was merely a question of relative efficacy. The main object of IRA attack was the Army and other security forces, who were in general well armed and protected. The only weapons which were of much use in this conflict were rifles and automatic weapons. The main object of attack for Protestant paramilitary associations, on the other hand, was the Roman Catholic population which was unarmed and undefended, and against which pistols and revolvers were as effective as rifles. It was clearly a matter of opinion whether attacks on the existence of the state were more serious than attacks on the minority civilian population. But the approach adopted by the judges was too close to that of the Protestant population at large to win acceptance from the minority.

Conclusions

A number of more general points may be made in conclusion to this chapter on the operation of the ordinary criminal courts in this period.

116

The first is that the progressive centralisation and professionalisation of the system of criminal justice, by the appointment of an independent Director of Public Prosecutions, the suspension of jury trial and the centralisation of all trials for serious terrorist offences in Belfast, did succeed in eliminating the more blatant forms of discrimination between Protestant and Roman Catholic defendants in the selection of charges, the granting of bail, the incidence of conviction and acquittal and the level of sentencing. This should have helped to create a greater degree of confidence in the administration of justice on the part of the minority, but the increasingly close and obvious connection between the judicial system and the state as the level of IRA violence increased served only to intensify the degree of alienation felt by many Roman Catholics. This was particularly the case in respect of the substantial difference in approach on the part of the authorities and the legal system to the IRA and to its counterparts in the Protestant community. The fact that this difference was founded in the concept that the state was fully entitled to take whatever measures to protect itself that were necessary and that the IRA offensive was in fact a greater threat to the state than the Protestant reaction to it did little to reassure the minority community given its deep-seated feeling as to the illegitimacy of that state.

The satisfactory operation of the system of criminal trials was also undermined by the superimposition of extra-judicial measures. Those who operated the judicial system and determined its reaction to the emergency conditions, both on a day-to-day basis and in the deliberations of the Diplock Committee, were committed to maintaining the established traditions and values of the common law in so far as was possible, with a view to minimising any loss of confidence in the ordinary courts. But they did little to prevent the adoption or control the operation of extra-judicial methods, in particular the system of dentention without trial and the practice of rearresting and detaining those who had been discharged by the courts. As a result, though the system of criminal trials did continue to operate effectively throughout the period of the emergency, it made little positive contribution to the restoration of order. The reasons for this are explored at greater length in the next chapter.

NOTES AND REFERENCES

1. *Report of the Commission to consider legal procedures to deal with terrorist activities in Northern Ireland* Cmnd. 5185, London 1972.
2. *Official Report* 855 H.C. Deb., col. 176, 17 April 1973.
3. These studies were financed by grants from the Legal Research Committee of the Law Faculty, Queen's University Belfast and by the Joseph Rowntree Trust; the results of the 1972 and 1973 surveys were published in *Justice in Northern Ireland: A Study in Social Confidence* by the Cobden Trust in October 1973, and those of the 1974 survey were included in the authors' submission to the Gardiner Committee in September 1974.
4. The details of the cases in each of these categories are given in the Appendix to *Justice in Northern Ireland.*
5. *Justice in Northern Ireland* Table 5.4.
6. For a more detailed account of the selection of firearms charges in this period see *Justice in Northern Ireland* and *Prosecutions in Northern Ireland: A Study of Facts* Law Officers' Department, London 1974; the differences in these two studies are discussed in Appendix A.
7. *Prosecutions in Northern Ireland* DPP Table A, p. 17; the figures for Roman Catholic defendants were supplied by those who compiled the official report.
8. *Justice in Northern Ireland* Table 5.5.
9. See generally 'The Minimum Sentences Act' by Kevin Boyle, *Northern Ireland Legal Quarterly* 1970, p. 425; the Act was repealed in August 1973.
10. *Official Report* 855 H.C. Deb., cols. 381–382, 17 April 1973.
11. *Prosecutions in Northern Ireland;* see further Appendix A.
12. *Prosecutions in Northern Ireland* Tables F and G, pp. 31–33.
13. *Justice in Northern Ireland* Table 5.7.
14. *Official Report* 855 H.C. Deb., col. 388, 17 April 1973.
15. *Official Report* H.C. Deb., Standing Committee B, col. 77, 8 May 1973.
16. Cmnd. 5185, London 1972.
17. A small number of scheduled offences tried for administrative reasons at the Belfast Recorder's Court in the same period were omitted.
18. See, for instance, *The American Jury* by Kalven and Zeisel, and *The Jury* by W. R. Cornish.
19. Kelly J. in *R. v. Tohill* Belfast City Commission, 6 March 1974.

7. PUBLIC CONFIDENCE IN THE ADMINISTRATION OF JUSTICE

Any institution in a liberal democratic state must have the confidence of the majority of the people if it is to operate successfully. The legal system is no exception. As long as public confidence in the legal system is maintained the authorities can deal with deviant and dissident members of society through the courts without either the procedures, principles or outcomes being questioned by the public or even by those being processed. In addition the belief that, when necessary, ordinary people may seek and obtain the redress of grievances through legal channels reduces the likelihood that they will resort to other more violent and disruptive means. The law not only provides for the smooth functioning of the state but ideally helps to preserve it by making unnecessary the use of naked force either by the authorities or by internal dissidents.

It is therefore in the interest of the authorities in liberal states to do everything in their power to preserve public confidence in every aspect of the legal system. Particular attention has to be paid to any criticism of the way in which the law is administered. When serious complaints are made, the authorities will normally respond by emphasising that the legal system is independent and that it upholds the principles of fairness and equality before the law. If they are wise they will also take action to remedy any obviously justifiable or widely held lack of confidence, though the extent of their response will depend on how widespread they perceive the lack of confidence to be and how great the threat to stability.

In an unstable society such as Northern Ireland where there is a continuing problem of legitimacy and a long history of violence and disorder, the authorities will always be faced with a dilemma in dealing with violence when it does break out. They may attempt to suppress it by relying on the ordinary legal system and hence be subject to the various constraints which the existing law imposes on them. Alternatively, they may seek to repress violence by whatever means they consider necessary regardless of legal constraints. This is likely to involve the rejection of values, principles and procedures deeply embedded in the conception of a liberal state.

One of these alternatives may be called the 'due process' response and the other the 'security' response. The effectiveness of each is highly problematic. The former may not curtail violence immediately but it is likely to leave unaffected the public's confidence in the legal system, thereby maintaining the legitimacy of the state. The second may seem more effective in the short term in dealing with violence but in the long term may prove to be counterproductive. Where the violence stems from deeply felt and widely held grievances, the security response is likely to cause further grievance. In these conditions it may also generate more widespread support for violent action. And at a deeper level it may have a damaging and lasting effect on public confidence in the legal system, and ultimately undermine the degree of acquiescence or support which is necessary for the preservation of a stable state.

There can be no doubt that from the creation of Northern Ireland the authorities chose the 'security' response and ignored the issue of public confidence. As has been seen, one of the first actions of the Unionist government was to introduce the Civil Authority (Special Powers) Act (Northern Ireland) in 1922 and to retain it in force, despite many years without internal or external disorders. When the control of the police was handed over to them by the Westminster government in 1922 the Unionists made no attempt to make it appear independent of government by establishing watch committees or similar organisations. Instead they made the Royal Ulster Constabulary directly answerable to the Minister of Home Affairs, and trained and organised the force along military lines.

In addition they maintained the Special Constabulary long after the disorders associated with the formation of the state had been quelled. As the majority of the members of the 'B Specials' were Loyalists, their very existence was a continual reminder to the minority that security could be expected to prevail over due process. Finally the Unionists adopted the policy of filling all but a few judicial posts with Protestants. Though the religious affiliation of a judge or magistrate did not normally affect the way in which justice was administered, the fact that the judiciary was not fully representative of both communities did little to inspire confidence in the impartiality of the legal system.

It is against this historical background that the account which follows of the problems of public confidence in the administration of justice during the current emergency must be seen. The first section attempts to demonstrate the extent of the distrust by the minority community in order to show the serious nature of the problem facing the authorities. This is followed by an analysis of the authorities' response to the situation, and in particular to the widespread allegations of misconduct and unlawful violence by the security forces. The chapter ends with an analysis of a small opinion survey conducted in August 1974 and designed specifically to test the validity of the assumptions pertaining to public confidence made by the Diplock Committee.

Public Concern by the Minority Community about the Administration of Justice

The most extensive public reaction by the minority community to the administration of justice was in relation to internment. There was outright condemnation of it when it was first introduced, particularly when it became known that only Roman Catholics had been picked up in the initial operation. The *Irish News,* the main organ of Roman Catholic opinion, commented:

> To ask as he (Faulkner) did yesterday for the co-operation of the Catholic Community in political affairs, after issuing orders for the arrest and internment of his political opponents is insincerity of the rankest sort. It is the hyprocrisy of Tartuffe. Yesterday was a day of awful tragedy.[1]

121

The Roman Catholic bishops, later in the month, added their criticism. Cardinal Conway stated that internment was a terrible power to give to a political authority. He also condemned its one-sided application. On a political level the opposition came from the Social Democratic and Labour Party, the Nationalist Party and civil rights bodies, which agreed on the following:

1) To call on those who held public positions to withdraw immediately.
2) To call on the general public to withhold rent and rates.
3) To give full support to all who call meetings to oppose internment.
4) To insist that the military resume the task that they were sent to Northern Ireland for – to protect people and areas against sectarian attacks.
5) To ask Westminster to suspend the system of government.

Opposition to internment, it should be noted, was not only voiced by members of the Roman Catholic community. The Rev. Ian Paisley, who had long been opposed to the use of internment, accused Mr Faulkner of using it as a weapon of purely political expediency to bolster up his own tottering premiership. The *Belfast Telegraph,* generally regarded as a non-aligned newspaper, commented that the situation could have been dealt with without introducing 'a legal monstrosity which was not only ineffective but which also caused hardship and injustice and in a sense was as unattractive as the situation it was meant to remedy'.[2]

Criticisms of other aspects of the administration of justice were equally vocal. In May 1971 the leaders of the main opposition party in the Stormont Parliament put down two motions, one calling for the removal from office of the Recorder of Belfast and the other censuring the Attorney-General, in each case on the ground of political bias in the administration of justice. In April 1971 a group of Roman Catholic priests refused to fill in their census forms as a protest against alleged discrimination in the courts. Father Faul, a Roman Catholic priest in Dungannon, who had published a number of statements on judicial matters, put it this way: 'Our people are afraid of the courts; they believe the judicial system as it operates in the blatantly sectarian conditions of life here is loaded against them.' After the introduction of internment without trial, a group of prominent Roman

Catholics made a comprehensive attack on the administration of justice:

> Criminal charges are preferred much more forcefully against Catholics than against any other section of the population, both in selecting the number and nature of the charges to be brought, in the seriousness or otherwise of the Act under which the charges are brought, the method of commencement of the charges (whether by arrest or by service of summons), in determining whether bail should be opposed and in collecting, selecting and presenting evidence to the courts.[3]

Concern over the administration of justice was not restricted to representatives of the Roman Catholic community in Northern Ireland. In May 1971 more than one hundred solicitors and barristers from both communities called on the Law Society and the Bar Council to set up an inquiry as a matter of urgency into the administration of the criminal law.

This general concern over the administration of justice covered all the various stages of the judicial process, from the choice of charges and the decision on bail to conviction and sentence.

On the choice of charge the main complaint was that Roman Catholics had been charged with more serious offences than Protestants for broadly similar behaviour. Allegations of this kind were especially prevalent following the enactment of the Criminal Justice (Temporary Provisions) Act (Northern Ireland) 1970, which made a six-month prison sentence mandatory for a long list of public order offences including riotous and disorderly behaviour. The statute was soon amended to exclude disorderly behaviour when it was found that a number of persons who had only been involved in domestic disputes were falling under the mandatory six-month sentence. But the amendment created an obvious means by which the police could determine the length of sentence to be imposed on defendants, and it was not long before allegations were made that Roman Catholics were being charged with riotous behaviour and Protestants with disorderly behaviour for similar conduct. In February 1971, for example, two bands of women assembled outside the Belfast Magistrates Court. One group were Roman Catholics, protesting against the prosecution of a man charged with wearing an IRA uniform at a funeral. Trouble broke out between these women and a group of Protestant counter-protesters; forty Roman Catholics were arrested and many charged with riotous behaviour. No Protestants were arrested. Six weeks later some 2000 Loyalists attempted to storm a Roman Catholic church in East Belfast. Only thirteen persons were arrested and only three were charged with riotous behaviour.

In respect of decisions on bail it was alleged that Protestants were more likely than Roman Catholics to be granted bail for similar offences. In 1970 a number of opposition MPs walked out of the Stormont Parliament following what they regarded as an unsatisfactory reply to a question about two apparently inconsistent bail decisions. In one case a Protestant charged with possessing a number of firearms was granted bail; in another a Roman Catholic charged with having a rusty firearm was remanded in custody. Even members of the judiciary publicly declared their concern over bail decisions. In January 1973 two County Court judges complained about lack of uniformity in bail decisions.[4] Soon after, a Resident Magistrate suggested that it was high time that the authorities formulated some policy on the granting of bail as a guide to the courts.[5]

Finally, there were frequent criticisms of decisions on conviction and sentence in particular cases. It was suggested that in riot cases magistrates were far too ready to accept the evidence of the security forces without question, and that Roman Catholics were more likely to be convicted than Protestants. On sentencing, comparisons of cases in which Roman Catholics were apparently dealt with more severely than Protestants were often made. In 1970 there was a public outcry when a Roman Catholic received a six-month sentence for writing 'no tea here' on a wall; this was compared with a case only a week later in which a former member of the B Specials received a suspended sentence of twelve months on four charges of unlawfully supplying guns. Again in April 1971 there was widespread concern at a case in which a Roman Catholic received a twelve-month jail sentence for shouting 'Up the IRA' on the fringes of a Protestant procession.

This lack of confidence in the complete impartiality of the courts was a continuing problem. In 1974 the Association for Legal Justice published on a monthly basis a number of brief analyses of cases heard in Diplock courts, and claimed that there was a continuing anti-Catholic bias in the courts, especially in the sentences imposed on Catholic defendants. In each month studied it was claimed that the average level of prison sentences imposed on Catholics (more than six years) was roughly double that imposed on Protestants (between three and four years).[6]

All these allegations received wide publicity in the local press. There can be no doubt that the result was to strengthen the longstanding distrust of the court system on the part of many Roman Catholics, and to reinforce their view that the whole of the security operation was being geared primarily to the suppression of Republican activity rather than to the impartial maintenance of law and order in Loyalist and Republican areas alike. The frequent references by both Unionist and British politicians to their successes in dealing with disorder and terrorism by judicial means were interpreted as little more than a propaganda exercise to conceal the basic bias in the system.

Official Reaction to the Question of Public Confidence

In the early stages of the civil rights campaign the question of public confidence in the judicial process was treated seriously. The report of the Hunt Committee on the reorganisation of the Royal Ulster Constabulary recognised that 'the impartiality of the police may be questioned if they are responsible for deciding who shall be prosecuted and thereafter for acting as prosecutor' and recommended the establishment of a system of independent public prosecutors on the Scottish model.[7] This recommendation was given further and more detailed consideration by the MacDermott Committee,[8] and eventually resulted in the creation of a new office of Director of Public Prosecutions for Northern Ireland with full responsibility for the selection and prosecution of all serious criminal charges and for advising the courts on bail applications throughout Northern Ireland. The first Director was appointed early in 1972, and progressively took over control of the situation. All cases tried on indictment, and all summary charges which had any direct or indirect connection with public disorder or terrorist activities, were dealt with by the Director's staff, though less serious cases, especially motoring offences, were still dealt with exclusively by the police. The Director was generally independent, but remained responsible to the Attorney-General of Northern Ireland for the due performance of his functions, a fact which raised some doubts as to the impartiality of decisions in relation to the prosecution of members of the security forces, as for instance in the case of the 'Bloody Sunday' shootings in Londonderry in January 1972.

Apart from these changes, the response of the authorities to allegations of bias in the judicial system was to emphasise the total impartiality of the judiciary, and to imply that anyone who criticised the courts was a politically motivated propagandist. A similar response was made to the widespread allegations of misconduct and unlawful violence by the security forces. The only serious attempt to look into the operation of the legal system as a whole was the study of the work of the Director of Public Prosecutions commissioned by the Attorney-General in response to the publication of the Cobden Trust report, *Justice in Northern Ireland.*[9] But even this largely ignored many of the basic issues of public confidence which that report raised. The rest of this section describes in detail how official attitudes failed to grasp the essential nature of the problem.

The Failure of Inquiries

At first the natural reaction to allegations of misconduct by the security forces was to call for official judicial inquiries. There were four major tribunals of inquiry into events in Northern Ireland: the Cameron Commission on Disturbances in Northern Ireland between October 1968 and March 1969;[10] the Scarman Tribunal on Violence and Civil Disturbances in Northern Ireland in 1969;[11] the Compton Inquiry into allegations against the security forces of physical brutality in Northern Ireland arising out of events in August 1971;[12] and the Widgery Tribunal on events on Sunday 30 January 1972 in Londonderry.[13] To these might be added the reports of the Parker Committee on methods of interrogation[14] and of the Diplock and the Gardiner Committees on the means of dealing with terrorists,[15] and the Scotland Yard investigation into the death of Samuel Devenny following the RUC incursions into the Bogside in April 1969.

Though there were complaints from committed factions on the thoroughness of the investigation conducted in some of these cases, it can hardly be doubted that those concerned did a reasonably good job, at least in eliciting the basic facts of what happened in the incidents into which they were inquiring. But equally it can hardly be doubted that the various inquiries failed completely in what was presumably one of their principal functions, that of restoring public confidence in the conduct of the security forces. Even if their intended purpose was to deflect public concern in the hope that the inevitable delay of the inquiry process would reduce the impact of the allegations of misconduct, the result was equally unsatisfactory. Four reasons may be given for this failure.

First, the terms of reference were usually interpreted in such a way as to exclude certain broader issues from the scope of inquiry. This was particularly true of the Widgery Tribunal, which was established by a Parliamentary motion to inquire ' . . . into a definite matter of urgent public importance, namely the events on Sunday 30 January which led to loss of life in connection with the procession in Londonderry on that day.' These terms were taken by Lord Widgery to exclude consideration of the important issues of Army/government relationships and the source of the orders for 30 January. Yet he devoted two full introductory pages to a description of the security situation in Londonderry over the previous six months, indicating the pressures under which the Army was operating. This was apparently based entirely on Army evidence. There was no similar description of the strains the people of Derry were experiencing. This one-sided approach to his terms of reference lessened the credibility of the rest of Lord Widgery's report.

Secondly, the conclusions which the various reports drew from their findings, with the possible exception of Cameron and Scarman, were not always in accord with what might have been expected from an objective assessment of those findings. The Compton Report, as explained in chapter 4, based its rejection of the allegations of brutality by security forces on a thoroughly unconvincing distinction between brutality and ill-treatment. Lord Widgery made a generally favourable assessment of the conduct of the paratroops in Londonderry which it is difficult to justify in terms of the specific findings he made over the various individual incidents with which he was concerned, notably the 'reckless' shooting in the Glenfada Flats area. And in reaching even these findings Lord Widgery appeared to have placed undue credence on Army evidence and to have distrusted all other sources. It was in any event the overall assessments of the various reports rather than the detailed findings which attracted most attention, and gave rise to the widespread feeling that the actions of the security forces were being 'whitewashed'. Assessments of this kind must remain a matter of opinion, but the Compton and Widgery reports certainly failed to persuade either the Roman Catholic community or uncommitted observers that their assessments had struck the right balance.

Thirdly, there was the question of delay. This applied primarily to the Scarman Tribunal which stretched over two whole years and finally reported nearly three years after the events into which it was inquiring. It is hardly surprising that after such a long delay the impact of the report was virtually nil in terms of restoring confidence in the impartiality of the RUC, in so far as that was a valid finding. By that time an entirely new set of disputed incidents and allegations had taken over from those of 1969.

Finally, and perhaps most important, was the fact that no action was taken to deal with those cases in which the various reports found the security forces or individual soldiers or policemen to have been seriously at fault. The most notorious instances in this respect were the findings of ill-treatment/brutality against those involved in the arrest, detention and interrogation of some of the persons arrested in August 1971, and the finding over the Glenfada Flats incidents, in which four civilians were shot dead, that on the balance of probability 'when these four men were shot the group of civilians was not acting aggressively and that the shots were fired without justification'.[16] It was widely agreed that in these cases the actions by the security forces constituted the criminal offences of assault or manslaughter, if not murder.

Yet no proceedings were authorised by the Attorney-General, despite a good deal of political pressure for such action to be taken. A similar comment may be made about the equally serious findings by Cameron and Scarman in respect of RUC and 'B Special' conduct in the earlier period, notably the shooting of John Gallagher in Armagh in August 1969, and the assaults on Samuel Devenny in Londonderry in April 1969. Neither of these cases, which for a long period received particular attention in allegations against the security forces, nor the many other less serious cases of proven misconduct, resulted in any public disciplinary action or sanctions against those responsible. Even when a full scale police investigation was instituted, as in the Devenny case, the sole result was a report that a conspiracy of silence within the RUC was preventing those responsible from being identified.

More generally the appointment of judges to chair what turned out to be essentially political inquiries blurred the distinction between executive and judicial functions, and had an adverse effect on public confidence in the impartial role of the latter. The cumulative effect was undoubtedly to destroy any feeling which may have existed that the appointment of an official inquiry would lead to justice being done.

The response of some sections of the community to the government's refusal to set up inquiries into a number of instances of alleged Army misconduct and the failure of official inquiries to reach satisfactory conclusions was to set up their own unofficial inquiries.[17] The first was the Gifford Inquiry set up in July 1971 following the shooting of Cusack and Beattie in Derry by the British Army. Lord Gifford, Paul O'Dwyer and Albie Sachs were asked to undertake an investigation of the incidents following refusal of an official inquiry other than a speedy and extended inquest. The Army authorities, despite two requests, refused to give evidence. The inquiry produced a very different account of the shootings from the official version, but no action was taken. The second unofficial inquiry was organised by Councillor Hugh Smith when the authorities refused to set up an official inquiry to investigate the shooting in the Shankill area of Belfast of two Protestants, McKinney and Johnston, in September 1972. It found that there was a *prima facie* case for charges of murder to be brought against the Parachute Regiment. The third unofficial inquiry was established under the auspices of the International League for the Rights of Man to assure a fair investigation of the killings and woundings in Londonderry on Bloody Sunday, 30 January 1972. The report, by Professor Dash from Philadelphia, was based on an analysis of the twenty volumes of official evidence at the official inquiry under Lord Widgery as well as hundreds of statements of civilian eye witnesses. Many of its conclusions differed from those of Lord Widgery. There have also been a number of less formal unofficial inquiries, for instance the investigation by Amnesty International of allegations of ill-treatment of detainees and a number of reports by the International Red Cross on conditions in Long Kesh. None of these inquiries achieved anything very specific or positive. Their prime significance is probably the fact that they were held at all.

Defensive Legal Action

The second phase in the response to alleged unlawful conduct by the security forces was the resort to legal action on behalf of those who claimed to have suffered injury or injustice. The initial impetus for this was undoubtedly provided by the internment and interrogation operations of August and September 1971, which had the effect of uniting the Roman Catholic community in opposition to current security policies. This brought general support from Roman Catholic lawyers to the idea of challenging the security forces in the courts. Much of the legal activity which ensued may be traced to the operation of the Association for Legal Justice, which brought together a number of lawyers and others in Belfast and set out to encourage the use of legal processes to deal with allegations against the security forces. Two broad forms of action were taken: first the use of procedural and technical defences based on misconduct by the security forces in cases where criminal charges had been brought against suspected terrorists; and secondly, the institution of direct civil and criminal proceedings against individual members of the security forces in respect of assaults, contested shooting incidents and other cases of unlawful activities by soldiers or the police. The record of the Northern Ireland judiciary in dealing with these cases was such as to dispel any reasonable suspicion of bias in favour of the security forces. But in almost every case, as will be seen, the response of the executive authorities was such that any possible beneficial effect in terms of public confidence in the courts was wholly or largely destroyed.

The first actions taken were a direct challenge to the legality of the whole internment operation. *Habeas corpus* proceedings were instituted in London in August 1971 in respect of two of those who had been arrested in the initial internment swoop and who were detained at that time in the prison ship Maidstone in Belfast Lough. The main ground of complaint was that it was beyond the power of the civil authorities in Northern Ireland to authorise the British Army to make arrests by regulations issued under the Special Powers Act. These test cases first came before Ackner J. who accepted jurisdiction but refused the applications on the merits, on the ground that Regulation 11, permitting members of Her Majesty's forces to make arrests without warrant, could not be said to constitute an infringement of the ban imposed by the Government of Ireland Act 1920 on legislation by the Northern Ireland Parliament in respect of the armed forces.[18] This decision was effectively upheld on appeal, though on the different ground that the British courts had had no jurisdiction to hear *habeas corpus* applications from Ireland since 1782 or 1783.[19]

When these writs of *habeas corpus* were further pursued in the High Court in Northern Ireland, as suggested by the British Court of Appeal, reliance was placed on the alternative ground that the men had not been properly informed of the grounds for their arrest, as discussed in chapter 4. But the challenge to the validity of regulations under the Special Powers Act conferring powers on the armed forces of the Crown was pursued in a later case, carefully selected for the purpose. The case arose out of the arrest of two Northern Ireland MPs for refusing to obey the order of an Army officer, purporting to act under a power conferred on him by Regulation 38 of the Special Powers Act

131

to disperse any public assembly. The defendants, who had been engaged in a sit-down demonstration against the behaviour of British troops in Derry, were convicted by the local magistrate, but won their appeal in the Northern Ireland High Court which held that in purporting to confer powers on the British Army the regulation sought to achieve a lawful object by unlawful means.[20] This decision clearly raised substantial doubts as to the legality of many other actions by the British Army taken under the Special Powers Act. But the basis of the decision was immediately removed by the Westminster Parliament by the enactment within a matter of hours of the Northern Ireland Act 1972. This specifically authorised the Northern Ireland Parliament to legislate in respect of the armed forces of the Crown in so far as that was necessary to the maintenance of peace and order in Northern Ireland, and conferred retrospective validity on any actions taken before the passing of the act which would otherwise have been invalid. The general opinion that the Special Powers Act could not be effectively challenged had been upheld once again, despite the tactical victory won on the interpretation of the regulation in question. In addition the hope that some assistance in the campaign against the wide terms of the Special Powers Act could be expected from the British Parliament had been finally disappointed.

The unchallengeable character of the Special Powers Act, however, did not prevent a number of other tactical victories based on ordinary common law rights being won on behalf of persons arrested and detained, or charged with criminal offences. The application for *habeas corpus* which had been originated in London was eventually granted in the Northern Ireland High Court on the ground that the applicant had not on his arrest been properly informed of the legal basis for that arrest as was required at common law: simply to inform him that he was being arrested under the Special Powers Act was not sufficient since his rights, if any, and his opportunity, if any, to meet and challenge the right of arrest exercised against him, differed according to which Regulation he was arrested under.[21] Since the identical form of words had been used by the Army in the case of all those arrested and detained during August and September 1971, this decision clearly meant that all the arrests were similarly unlawful.

The practical effect of this decision, however, was less far-reaching than might appear. There was nothing to prevent the authorities from remedying the technical defect by formally arresting all those concerned. The complainant himself was formally released by order of the Court, but was rearrested and detained on leaving Belfast Prison. The net result in most cases was thus merely to open the way for civil action against the authorities for unlawful imprisonment for the period of the unlawful detention. In one test case involving the unlawful detention of a young unmarried student for just over a month it was held that a sum of £400 would be adequate compensation.[22] In another bizarre case involving a criminal charge of escaping from prison it was held that the invalidity of the accused person's arrest necessarily destroyed the basis of the charge, since to escape from unlawful custody was not an offence.[23] But the more immediate and emotive issue of the continued detention of those concerned was not affected.

The practical effect of a number of other tactical legal victories in the period following the internment and interrogation operations may similarly be questioned. The judges of the High Court did not hesitate to apply the common law as to the admissibility of confessions to exclude any statements obtained by improper pressures on those accused. In one case the authorities admitted that the defendant had been kept in a tiny cubicle with room only for a wooden chair and questioned at intervals throughout the day and night for a period of twenty-four hours. The judge rejected any allegations of physical ill-treatment but held that 'the circumstances in which this accused was detained and which preceded the making of this statement were such as to tend to sap . . . that free will which must exist before a confession is voluntary', and refused to admit the statement.[24] In another case in which the facts were not reported the Lord Chief Justice refused to admit confessions on the ground that 'the interrogation set-up was officially organised and operated in order to obtain information . . . from persons who would otherwise have been less willing to give it'.[25]

Procedural decisions of this kind frequently resulted in directed acquittals or the withdrawal of formal charges against accused persons. The Attorney-General stated in Parliament in April 1973 that there had been '55 abandoned cases, *nolle prosequis,* in Belfast since the beginning of 1972 mainly because of the inadmissibility of confession statements'; he also referred to 39 cases in which charges of possession of arms or explosives were withdrawn or the defendants discharged because of the technical rule that where premises are shared by several persons the prosecution must prove conclusively which of those persons was responsible for, or at least knew of, the presence of arms or explosives.[26]

These defensive victories, however, did not always lead to the release of the defendant. There were numerous cases in which the power to arrest and detain under the Special Powers Act was used to 'correct' what were viewed by the authorities as merely technical defects. The most striking of these cases were those in which persons acquitted or discharged on all charges against them were rearrested at the doors of the courts. Similar action was taken in February 1972 in the case of a man who had won an appeal against his original conviction on the ground of a misdirection to the jury. Court decisions on bail were also ignored by the authorities. In one well publicised case a Resident Magistrate decided that there was no case to answer on six of the seven charges brought against a Mr Close in respect of a shooting incident some weeks prior to his arrest in August 1971, and ordered his release on bail; yet Mr Close was immediately taken back into custody under the existing (and technically invalid) detention order against him; it was not until further *habeas corpus* proceedings had been instituted in the High Court, in the course of which the judge condemned the authorities in the strongest terms for acting 'with scant regard for the law and the liberty of the subject', that Mr Close was actually released.[27] Yet when he later answered to his bail, he was detained at the close of the day's proceedings and his solicitor denied access to him until his release just before midnight. The remaining charge against him was finally dismissed for want of evidence by direction of the trial judge.[28]

The net effect of the stand taken by the judges on the common law rights of accused persons was thus a good deal less significant than might be assumed. Some small benefits may have been

134

conferred on those concerned, for instance by the decision that the common law rules of natural justice required that all interned persons appearing before the advisory committee set up under the Special Powers Act should be provided with a written summary of the information on which suspicion against them was based, and also that they might be represented by a lawyer if they so wished.[29] Even in this respect, however, the court felt obliged to make an exception in any case where the disclosure of the relevant information would be contrary to public safety either by prejudicing the work of the security forces or by revealing their intelligence system. Similarly in the confession cases the courts were careful to emphasise that it was not for them to interfere with the processes of interrogation. The strict application of the common law rules on arrest, on the admissibility of confessions, and on natural justice may have salved the conscience of the judges in matters of this kind, but it did not generally make any great practical difference to the treatment of individual suspects, given the absolute power vested in the authorities by the Special Powers Act and the Emergency Provisions Act to detain any person they pleased. The general effect on public confidence in the judicial system of the continual superimposition by the security forces of 'executive justice' when the decisions of the courts displeased them can scarcely be overestimated.

Civil Actions Against the Authorities

A second line of attack in the attempt to use legal means to prevent misconduct by the security forces was the institution of direct actions for damages against the individual soldiers or policemen alleged to have acted unlawfully or against the authority responsible for their conduct. The eventual outcome in many of these civil actions was reasonably satisfactory. But once again the response of the authorities was often such as to offset the beneficial effect which a rapid settlement of the claims might have had.

In the first place the authorities frequently gave the appearance of using every means at their disposal to discourage the initiation of proceedings, and the initial cases were strenuously contested. In a widely publicised test case arising out of the alleged ill-treatment of those arrested and detained on 9 August 1971 the authorities first sought to block the proceedings by objecting to the disclosure of information necessary to the plaintiff's case, and to the admission of evidence by affidavit on his behalf. When it was replied that the plaintiff had gone to live in the Republic for fear of being rearrested, they refused to give any undertaking that if the plaintiff did appear in person he would be given a safe conduct. Eventually after a protracted series of preliminary hearings the County Court judge agreed to admit the affidavits, and made the following comment:

> In the absence of explanation or evidence from the defendants [I] make the *prima facie* inference that the defendants are relying on the plaintiff's fear as a tactic to postpone the hearing of this claim and that *prima facie* they do not *bona fide* desire production of the plaintiff for cross examination.

After a lengthy trial the judge found for the plaintiff in his action for assault, trespass or battery of the person and awarded him £300 damages, the maximum figure which he could legally give. In the course of his judgment he made further remarks which are indicative of the attitude of the authorities at the time:

> There is a deafening silence from the RUC (generally), and anybody of Army rank higher than Lieutenant Barton (who admits he is the Senior Officer referred to in paragraph 152 of the Compton Report) as to what went on in the huts, and how and why the procedures which admittedly did develop there were allowed to do so, and why the circumstances in which the men were kept were so primitive notwithstanding the duty of the defendants under the regulations. The urgency of the decision to arrest may be a reason but not a justification. I take the view that the very primitive circumstances must have been foreseen by commanders of greater seniority than Lieutenant Barton, that the entire pattern . . . was one of authority, rigid discipline and regimentation . . . and was preconceived. . . . This course was adopted irrespective of whether the people were guilty or innocent, or the relative gravity of matter available in each case to create suspicion.[30]

There can be little doubt that the attitude of the authorities in cases such as this went far beyond legitimate defence tactics in an

136

adversary system and gave support to the belief that the security forces were anxious to deter or prevent the initiation of proceedings against them whenever possible.

Second, there was the question of delay. In the aftermath of the arms searches and curfew in the Lower Falls area early in July 1970 the Army made a point of asking those who had suffered material damage to their homes to seek compensation through the official channels. But it was not until 1 December that a test case came before the Belfast Recorder's Court, reportedly the first occasion on which a compensation order under the Special Powers Act had been made. In a similar test case involving a Mr Kelly, a student who had been arrested in place of his brother on 9 August 1971, and who claimed damages for unlawful detention, it was not until 11 January 1973 that the case was finally disposed of by the award of £400 and costs in the High Court. It was held that while in the circumstances Mr Kelly's detention could not be held to have been unreasonable, and while he had not suffered any ill-treatment or any special distress from being confined with persons of different political views from his own, he had not been properly informed of the grounds for his arrest and was entitled to damages in respect of 'arrest in the middle of the night, the vexation and perhaps humiliation of the circumstances of his arrest in the presence of his recently re-united family, the interrogation and frustration and deprivation necessarily involved in prison life, not knowing when or how its term would expire'.[31] In another case arising out of a notorious incident in which a housewife's eyes had been put out by a discharge of a rubber bullet through her window at point blank range on 4 November 1971, it was not until 19 March 1973 that the Ministry of Defence, while still denying liability, agreed to pay £35,000 in compensation.

Delays of this length are commonplace in civil actions for personal injury. But in cases where misconduct by the security forces was alleged there was a special need for speed if confidence in the availability of legal redress was to be maintained. The figures given by the Attorney-General in April 1973 were indicative of the general lack of urgency on the part of the authorities: of the 150 civil claims against the Crown in cases of alleged ill-treatment by the security forces, only 39 had been settled by that date.[32] Specially expedited procedures were introduced to deal with compensation payments for businesses affected by terrorist explosions, but there was no similar scheme to ensure the speedy settlement of disputed incidents involving the security forces.

Criminal Prosecution

The belated satisfaction which might eventually be obtained in a civil action was also offset by the knowledge that no penalty was thereby imposed on those responsible for the unlawful action. This fact, and the desire among some members of the minority community to avenge what appeared to them to be the wholly unjustifiable conduct of some soldiers and policemen, led to calls for criminal charges to be laid in respect of some of the more serious incidents, in particular those in which it had been alleged that persons arrested had been deliberately beaten up in the course of interrogation or innocent civilians deliberately shot by Army patrols. It was revealed by the Attorney-General in April 1973 that there had been demands for criminal prosecution against thirty-seven members of the security forces for inflicting bodily harm and sixty-two cases of unlawful shooting, malicious damage and larceny.[33]

The legal position in such cases was relatively straightforward. Since members of the security forces were in exactly the same position in law as anyone else, except in so far as special powers of arrest and questioning were conferred on them, any physical injury inflicted by a soldier or policeman deliberately and without lawful justification would constitute a criminal offence. Where the complainant was simply pushed around, a charge of common assault might be laid; where he suffered real physical injury, as in the cases of alleged beatings, a charge of aggravated assault or malicious or felonious wounding might be laid; and where the victim was killed or seriously injured by gunfire, a charge of manslaughter, murder or attempted murder might be laid.

The definition of 'lawful justification' for this purpose depends largely on the common law conception of what is reasonable in

138

the circumstances and in relation to the complainant's own conduct. Reasonable force may be applied, for instance, to prevent escape from lawful custody or to prevent the commission of a crime. In respect of the use of weapons in Northern Ireland, these rules were clearly and precisely stated in the yellow card issued to every soldier. The card set out the circumstances in which soldiers might lawfully open fire: for instance 'against a person carrying a firearm, but only if you have reason to think that he is about to use it for offensive purposes and he refuses to halt when called upon to do so . . .'; or 'if there is no other way to protect yourself or those whom it is your duty to protect from the danger of being killed or seriously injured'. Though some changes were made in the wording on the yellow card from time to time, the validity of the rules contained in it as an accurate statement of the common law rights of the armed forces was not seriously questioned. Accordingly, if it could be shown that in a particular case the rules in the yellow card had not been followed, that would be *prima facie* evidence that an offence had been committed, subject always to the possible defence of reasonable mistake. Allegations that soldiers had not adhered to the rules in the yellow card were frequently made, for instance in the cases of the shooting of three alleged bank robbers in Newry in October 1971, the civilians shot dead in Derry on 'Bloody Sunday' in January 1972, and those shot dead in the Ardoyne area of Belfast in the spring of 1973. Cases in which admitted members of the IRA were shot dead, as in the case of Joe McCann in the Markets area of Belfast in the spring of 1972, raised more difficult issues, but here too it was probably unlawful for soldiers to shoot to kill merely to prevent escape.[34]

However, relatively few of the cases in which demands for criminal prosecution against members of the security forces were made came before the courts and in those which did the result seldom proved satisfactory to the complainants. In a number of cases the defendants were acquitted, either at the original trial or on appeal. In one important case arising out of a fatal shooting in Newry, a conviction against a soldier on a charge of manslaughter was quashed on appeal on the ground that the evidence was unsatisfactory.[35] In other cases charges were not pursued beyond a certain point. In others it proved impossible to gain the assistance of the prosecuting authorities, as for instance in the cases arising out of the Bloody Sunday shootings. There was accordingly a widespread belief among members of the minority community that it was futile to attempt to pursue a serious criminal charge against the security forces. The various reasons for this belief and their validity are worth considering in some detail.

First there was the practical difficulty of initiating criminal proceedings, particularly prior to the establishment of the Director of Public Prosecutions in 1972. In theory there was nothing to prevent ordinary individuals from exercising their common law right to initiate private prosecutions. But in practice this was not easy to do. One problem in cases involving the security forces was the identification of the particular policeman or soldier involved. In coroner's courts military and police witnesses, for obvious reasons, were identified only by a letter. Another problem was that the coroner's courts in Northern Ireland could not bring in any verdict which implied that a criminal offence was involved in the death. This restriction effectively prevented a coroner or his jury from putting pressure on the authorities to initiate criminal proceedings by entering a verdict of murder or manslaughter where that appeared *prima facie* to be a justifiable inference. Some of these difficulties could have been surmounted by the effective use of such standard legal procedures as an application for discovery of the identity of a particular soldier. But no private prosecution was in fact initiated. It was not until the new office of Director of Public Prosecutions was set up, with the express duty of looking into cases referred by private individuals, that any serious criminal charges were laid against members of the security forces.

Secondly, there was the problem of collecting evidence. Again it was theoretically possible for a private individual or lawyer to undertake this. But in cases where the Army was involved or ballistic evidence was required, official co-operation was a practical necessity. In any event, there was a tendency for complainants to expect any necessary investigation to be carried out for them by the police, and then to complain that inquiries had not been pursued by the police with sufficient vigour, allegedly with the ulterior motive of preventing any proceedings being

140

started. Some of this apparent lack of vigour was due to the insistence by the Army that questioning of Army personnel should be carried out by the military police. Quite apart from the appearance of partiality which this rule created, the division of an investigation between civilian and military police was not calculated to increase its efficacy. More seriously, there were allegations that witnesses of some of the more serious shooting incidents had been deliberately harassed and even shot at by soldiers to deter them from giving evidence which might lead to a conviction, as in the case of a civilian shot dead by the Paratroop Regiment in the Ardoyne area in April 1973. Finally, there was the natural tendency of soldiers and policemen to seek to cover up any misconduct by their colleagues.

The results in those cases which came to court after the Director of Public Prosecutions had taken charge bore out some of these complaints and allegations. In a case heard in October 1972 involving charges of assault against two police constables and two soldiers, in which the jury brought verdicts of simple assault against the soldiers only, the judge made the following comments:

> I find this case unsatisfactory in the way it was presented to the court. It is a matter of great importance, and it is clear that Hughes was assaulted very badly while he was in the custody of the security forces. It is clear that this court has not heard anything like the truth about the matter. I am satisfied that there has been a conspiracy of silence on the part of some people, and I am directing that the papers be sent to the Attorney-General.[36]

Similar problems arose in a case against two detectives and a soldier alleged to have beaten up three men arrested and interrogated in Belfast in April 1972. It was clear from the medical evidence that someone must have given the complainants a severe beating. The defence case was that the men must have been beaten by unknown Army personnel before being presented for questioning. In the event the judge directed that the case against the soldiers should be dismissed, and the two detectives were found not guilty by the jury.[37] Some cases resulted in convictions. It was reported in May 1973 that since December 1970 twenty-nine soldiers had been tried for offences against

civilians: fourteen out of twenty-five had been convicted of
simple assault but only one out of four of the more serious
simple assault but only one out of four of the more serious
offence of wounding.[38] A further set of official figures for the
period March 1972 to September 1974 showed an equally low
conviction rate:

	Cases investigated by prosecuting authorities	Prose-cutions ordered	Result			
			with-drawn	pend-ing	acquit-ted	con-victed
Army and UDR	502	56	3	15	21	17
Police	407	10	–	3	7	–

Most of the convictions were for minor off-duty offences, such
as public house brawls. The more serious charges of unlawful
violence by soldiers on duty or by those conducting interrogations rarely led to a conviction.

This pattern is not difficult to explain in the broader
perspective of the security operation as a whole. Any legal system
may be expected to apply the very strictest standards in dealing
with cases in which members of the police, the prosecuting
authorities or the judiciary are accused of unlawful conduct.
The chances of securing a conviction are correspondingly less.
This tendency is likely to be strengthened in an emergency situation, particularly when, as in Northern Ireland, the security
forces are brought in from outside. The political pressures on
the Westminster government to reassure the British public that
the Army was doing a good job in Ulster were very strong, and
the temptation to excuse or explain away any proven misconduct
very great. To permit the conviction of a soldier on any serious
criminal charge, which necessarily involved the proof of a
deliberate or reckless breach of the law, would constitute a
serious breach of the officially sponsored image. There were
similar internal pressures on the authorities in Northern Ireland
from the Protestant community to protect members of the police
and local security forces. As in the case of interrogation techniques and internment, discussed in chapters 4 and 5, it is
arguable that the government would have been better advised
in the long term to resist such pressures and place more emphasis

on seeking to maintain the confidence of the Roman Catholic community in the legal system as a whole. But its failure to do so should not be regarded as in any way unexpected or abnormal.

Public Attitudes to the System of Detention and to Diplock Courts

The insensitivity of the authorities to the lack of confidence by many sections of the community in the administration of justice was most clearly seen in the deliberations of the Diplock Committee. The Committee's recommendations in December 1972 were based on a set of clearly expressed assumptions about public attitudes in Northern Ireland. The first of these was that the judiciary in Northern Ireland had maintained a reputation for impartiality which rose above the divisive conflict between the two rival communities:

> Northern Ireland has always been a province whose inhabitants have been sharply divided into two rival factions by differences of creed and politics. The judiciary has nevertheless managed to retain a reputation for impartiality which rises above the divisive conflict which has affected so many other functions of government in the province; and the courts of law and the procedures that they use have in general held the respect and trust of all except the extremists of both factions. We regard it as of paramount importance that the criminal courts of law and judges and resident magistrates who preside in them should continue to retain that respect and trust throughout the emergency and after the emergency has come to an end. If anything were done which weakened it, it might take generations to rebuild, for in Northern Ireland memories are long (para. 13).

The Committee went on to infer that any derogation from ordinary procedures for criminal trials which interfered too radically with accepted common law values should be avoided for fear that the ordinary courts would become tainted with the lack of respect and trust which might accompany special provision for dealing with terrorists. The second assumption was that the maintenance of an entirely separate procedure for the administrative detention of terrorists would not affect public attitudes to the ordinary courts.

The preceding sections in this chapter suggest that these assumptions were unjustified, and that much of the basic thinking and strategy of the Diplock Committee was misguided and likely to be counterproductive. Further evidence for this was provided by a small survey of public attitudes directed specifically to testing the validity of the assumptions made by the Diplock Committee.

The survey was carried out in Belfast in August 1974. The sample was composed of 180 persons selected on a quota basis to reflect the distribution of age, sex, class and religion in the whole of Belfast. The interviews were conducted by a small team of interviewers mainly in areas which were regarded as troubled. Of the 180 persons interviewed 118 were Protestants, 57 Roman Catholics, and the remainder were neither. The results from a small quota sample of this kind must obviously be treated with a great deal of caution, but they do provide an indication of the nature of public attitudes to the legal system in Northern Ireland.

The survey was primarily intended to ascertain people's opinions on internment, the Commissioners' hearings, the quality of justice being dispensed by the ordinary courts and the abolition of juries. It also attempted to ascertain to what extent people perceived the operation of internment as separate from the operation of the ordinary courts, and whether internment was affecting public confidence in the operation of the ordinary courts of law. As opinion is dependent on knowledge, it was also necessary to find out the extent of the respondents' knowledge of the changes introduced in 1972 and 1973.

Knowledge of changes in legal procedures
The figures in Table 7.1 indicate that a sizeable proportion of the community in Belfast did know about the changes in the administration of justice introduced in the Emergency Provisions Act. Though there was some difference between the two communities nearly half the sample knew about the introduction of the new system of Commissioners' hearings in internment cases and two-thirds knew about the abolition of juries.

144

TABLE 7.1:   *Knowledge of certain changes in the system of detention and the courts*

| | Protestant | | Roman Catholic | |
	No.	%	No.	%
Number who knew about the Commissioners	59	50	21	37
Number who knew about the abolition of juries	74	63	45	79

Opinions on internment

Table 7.2 shows that nearly two-thirds of those interviewed were opposed to internment. But there was a substantial difference between the views of Protestants and Roman Catholics. Only half of the Protestants interviewed were opposed to internment while nearly every Roman Catholic was opposed to it. Protestant opposition varied between age groups – the men in the 18–24 age group were most against it – but there was little variation between the sexes and between classes.

TABLE 7.2:   *Reasons for opposing or agreeing with internment*

| | Protestant | | Roman Catholic | |
	No.	%	No.	%
Reasons for opposing internment:				
1. Legal injustice	10	8	1	2
2. Political injustice	2	2	17	30
3. Immoral	1	1	21	37
4. Protestant appeasement	–	–	2	3
5. Other or unstated	43	36	13	23
Total opposed	56	47	54	95
Reasons for agreeing with internment:				
1. Pragmatism	22	19	1	2
2. Other or unstated	40	34	2	4
Total in agreement	62	53	3	6
Total number of respondents	118	100	57	100

The nature of the opposition to or agreement with internment varied. But as less than one-third of all respondents gave a reason for holding a particular viewpoint on internment any analysis of the reasons must be treated with caution. Of the thirteen Protestants who gave reasons for opposing internment, ten gave a reason which could be classified under the heading 'legal injustice'. This included all replies which referred to some legal shortcomings in the internment process, as for example: 'everyone should be tried'; 'should be a trial wherever possible'; 'everyone should be given a trial'. Of those who agreed with internment, all did so for what were classified as pragmatic reasons, as for example: 'very unjust but necessary in the circumstances'; 'keep it if it keeps the trouble down'; 'have to stay until violence stops'; 'under present circumstances a necessary evil'.

The reasons for Roman Catholic opposition to internment could be classified into two broad groups. The first included all comments which made an implicit or explicit political comment on internment, as for example: 'disgrace in any democratic state'; 'totally unjustified form of state oppression'; 'condemn it utterly as a repressive measure used only by a police state'. The second group included all answers which suggested that internment was immoral, for example, 'it's unchristian'; 'it is immoral'. Some 30 per cent of Catholic respondents gave the first reason and 37 per cent the second. A few others suggested that it was introduced to please the Unionist or Loyalist community; these were labelled 'Protestant appeasement'.

The analysis in Table 7.3 of the reasons of both Protestants and Roman Catholics for opposing or agreeing with the system of Commissioners' hearings on internment cases produced a similiar set of responses but in different proportions. Protestant opposition to the process was again based mainly on legal grounds whereas Roman Catholics raised political and moral objections. Only one Roman Catholic agreed with the system; Protestant agreement was based on pragmatic grounds. Again only a small proportion of respondents gave reasons and their opinions may not be representative of the opinions of the whole sample.

The survey also indicated that the existence of internment had adversely affected confidence in the ordinary courts. Table 7.4

shows that two out of every three persons interviewed thought that internment had decreased people's confidence in the courts. More than half of the Protestant respondents and nearly all the Roman Catholic respondents held this view.

TABLE 7.3: *The number of Protestants and Roman Catholics who knew of the Commissioners and their reasons for opposing or agreeing with the process*

	Protestant		Roman Catholic	
	No.	%	No.	%
Reasons for opposing it:				
1. Legal injustice	19	32	6	28
2. Political injustice	–	–	6	28
3. Other or unstated	12	20	8	38
Total opposed	31	52	20	94
Reasons for agreeing with it:				
1. Pragmatism	10	17	–	–
2. Other or unstated	18	30	1	5
Total agreed	28	47	1	5
Total number of respondents	59	100	21	100

TABLE 7.4: *The views of Protestants and Roman Catholics on the effects of internment on people's confidence in the ordinary courts*

	Protestant		Roman Catholic	
	No.	%	No.	%
Increased	17	14	1	2
Decreased	70	59	53	93
No change	10	9	3	5
No opinion	21	18	–	–
Total	118	100	57	100

Opinions on the trial process

The respondents were also asked to give a general opinion on the performance of the ordinary courts. Most Protestants stated that they thought people got a fair trial in the courts, as shown in Table 7.5. A variety of reasons were given by those Protestants who believed that a person did not get a fair trial: half suggested

TABLE 7.5: *The number of Protestants and Roman Catholics who thought that a person did not get a fair trial in Northern Ireland and their reasons for holding this view*

	Protestant		Roman Catholic	
	No.	%	No.	%
Number who think that a person does not get a fair trial in Northern Ireland:	32	27	50	88
Reasons:				
1. Biased or inconsistent sentences	16	50	4	8
2. Biased against Roman Catholics	3	9	44	88
3. Biased against Protestants	3	9	–	–
4. Absence of due process	5	16	–	–
5. Other or unstated	5	16	2	4
Total number of respondents	32	100	50	100

TABLE 7.6: *The number of Protestants and Roman Catholics who knew about the abolition of juries for scheduled offences and their reasons for opposing or agreeing with the change*

	Protestant		Roman Catholic	
	No.	%	No.	%
Number who knew about the abolition of juries:	74	63	45	79
Reasons for opposing:				
1. Legal injustice	13	17	3	7
2. Political injustice	–	–	5	11
3. Other or unstated	19	26	16	35
Total opposing	32	43	24	53
Reasons for agreeing:				
1. Pragmatism	13	18	2	4
2. Intimidation of jurors	9	12	–	–
3. Prejudiced/biased jurors	5	7	2	4
4. Other or unstated	10	13	12	27
Total agreeing	37	50	16	35
No opinion	5	7	5	11
Total number of respondents	74	100	45	100

that sentences were inconsistent; others stated that the trials were unfair because juries had been abolished or because of the existence of the system of detention; some thought the courts were biased against Protestants. Roman Catholics were nearly unanimous in thinking that a person could not get a fair trial because the courts were biased against Catholics.

Further information on the trial process was obtained by asking about the abolition of juries. As shown in Table 7.6, the reaction to the change among those Protestants who knew about it was mixed: half were in agreement and most of the rest were opposed. Those in agreement justified it either in general terms, for instance that it was necessary in the situation, or more specifically in that it overcame the problems of intimidation of jurors or prejudiced juries. Those opposing the change again raised the legal objection that it violated normally accepted procedures.

The Roman Catholic respondents were not so evenly divided: for every three opposing the change, there were two in agreement with it. In addition there was less consensus of opinion than on other issues. Those agreeing to the change did so, generally, on the grounds that it overcame the problem of prejudiced juries. The majority of those opposed gave no reason. One explanation for this lack of consensus among Roman Catholics on this issue may be that they were placed in a dilemma. On the one hand they saw the abolition as overcoming the problem of prejudice, but on the other they may have had grave doubts about the impartiality of the judges who were replacing the juries.

Perception of the interrelationship between the courts and internment

To explore whether or not people perceived the operation of the ordinary courts and internment as two distinct processes the respondents were asked the question 'What difference, if any, do you see between a person convicted in the courts and a person detained by the commissioners?' As shown in Table 7.7, two out of every three Protestants replied that there was a difference: the majority suggested that the principal difference was the way in which the person was convicted; many said that a person tried in the courts was more likely to be guilty. But Roman Catholics

149

made no such distinction: almost all stated that there was no difference. The following were some of the replies: 'courts are used as a semi-respectable form of internment therefore there is no difference'; 'both are victims of state violence therefore there is no difference'; 'one is an extension of the other'; 'no difference – both are methods of putting people away'.

TABLE 7.7: *The views of Protestants and Roman Catholics on the differences, if any, between persons convicted in the courts and those detained by the Commissioners*

	Protestant No.	Protestant %	Roman Catholic No.	Roman Catholic %
1. Differences in legal process	73	62	5	9
2. Difference – other or unstated	6	5	3	5
Total suggesting differences	79	67	8	14
1. No difference in systems	–	–	10	17
2. No difference in persons	7	6	–	–
3. No difference – other or unstated	23	19	39	68
Total suggesting no differences	30	25	49	86
Don't know	9	7	–	–
Total number of respondents	118	100	57	100

Conclusion

The results of this small survey, showing the essentially different approach of members of the majority and minority communities to the operation of the legal system, go some way to explain the dilemma facing the authorities – that while the Protestant community was prepared to countenance changes in the legal system designed to deal with the emergency situation, the Roman Catholic community regarded any derogation from ordinary rules of law as further proof of their view that the legal system was part and parcel of an oppressive state. The account of the civil rights struggle in chapter 2 and the rest of the material in this chapter suggest that this was a longstanding problem, in the sense that the minority community never really trusted the legal institutions of the state in which they lived. But as the level of disorder and violence increased, and the authorities moved progressively from a due process to a security approach, the problem became progressively more acute. The security approach in itself involved greater concentration on practical results than on matters of public confidence, and made it less and less likely that the kind of impartial inquiry into disputed incidents which public confidence demanded would be forthcoming, or that those responsible for misconduct would be effectively dealt with. In most states this would not be a matter for lasting concern, since security operations are normally directed against a tiny minority. But in Northern Ireland, where the minority community was large enough to make its continued support for or at least its acquiescence in the legal system as a whole essential to the stability of the state, it could only make matters worse.

NOTES AND REFERENCES:

1. *Irish News* 10 August 1971.
2. *Belfast Telegraph* 9 August 1971.
3. *Commentary upon the White Paper* (*Command Paper 558*) *entitled 'A Record of Constructive Change'* Belfast 1971.
4. *Belfast Telegraph* 8 January 1973.
5. *Belfast Telegraph* 10 January 1973.
6. Association for Legal Justice *Anti-Catholic Bias in the Courts of Northern Ireland* Sample Studies, March, April and May–June 1974.
7. *Report of the Advisory Committee on Police in Northern Ireland* Cmd. 535, Belfast 1969, para. 142.
8. *Report of the Working Party on Public Prosecutions* Cmd. 554, Belfast 1971.
9. *Prosecutions in Northern Ireland: A Study of Facts* Law Officers' Department, London 1974.
10. Cmd. 532, Belfast 1969.
11. Cmd. 566, Belfast 1972.
12. Cmnd. 4823, London 1971.
13. H.C. 220, April 1972.
14. Cmnd. 4901, London 1972.
15. Cmnd. 5185, London 1972.
16. H.C. 220, para. 85.
17. *Inquiry into the circumstances surrounding the deaths of Seamus Cusack and George Desmond Beattie,* Northern Ireland Socialist Research Centre, 1972; *Justice Denied: A Challenge to Lord Widgery's Report on Bloody Sunday* by Samuel Dash, Defence and Education Fund of the International League for the Rights of Man in association

with National Council for Civil Liberties, 1972; for details of the Shankill inquiry see *Irish Times* 11 September 1972.

18. *The Times* 2 September 1971.
19. *In re Keenan & Another* [1971] 3 W.L.R. 844.
20. *R. v. JPs for the County of the City of Londonderry, ex parte Hume and Others* 23 February 1972.
21. *In re McElduff* 12 October 1971.
22. *Kelly v. Minister of Home Affairs* 11 January 1973.
23. *R. v. Meehan* January 1973.
24. *R. v. Gargan* 10 May 1972.
25. *R. v. Flynn & Leonard* 24 May 1972.
26. 855 H.C. Deb., col. 388, 17 April 1973.
27. *In re Close* 22 December 1971.
28. 'The Rule of Law in Northern Ireland' by Tom Hadden, *New Law Journal* 17 February 1972, p. 161.
29. *In re Mackey* 16 December 1971.
30. *Moore v. Shillington and Minister of Defence* Armagh County Court, 3 January and 18 February 1972.
31. *Kelly v. Minister of Home Affairs* 11 January 1973.
32. 855 H.C. Deb., col. 388, 17 April 1973.
33. 855 H.C. Deb., col. 388, 17 April 1973.
34. For a more detailed discussion see 'The Myths of Martial Law' by Tom Hadden, *Fortnight* 29 October 1971.
35. *R. v. Foxford* 15 March 1974.
36. *Irish Times* 18–19 October 1972.
37. *Irish News* 14–17 March 1973.
38. 856 H.C. Deb., Written Answers, col. 201, 11 May 1973.

8. INTERNATIONAL PROCEEDINGS

One of the most entrenched assumptions of international relations is that an independent state has the right to settle its domestic affairs, including its form of government, as it sees fit. Since the creation of the United Nations Organisation, and the growth of economic and political interdependence of states, this traditional concept of sovereignty has been gradually eroded.

The efforts in the post-war world to commit governments to the protection of basic human rights within their territories through international treaties is one reflection of the new inter-state relationships. Of these treaties the European Convention on Human Rights, to which the United Kingdom government along with sixteen other European nations is a signatory, is recognised as the most advanced in terms of individual rights guaranteed and enforcement machinery. Since the onset of the conflict in Northern Ireland the provisions of the European Convention have frequently been invoked, and while it is difficult to assess the impact of this system of 'external' law on events, the various occasions on which its protections have been sought, as well as the response of government policy and security activity to them, deserve consideration.

The Machinery of the European Convention

The Convention came into force in September 1953 when the signatory states agreed to ensure protection through their domestic law of certain rights and freedoms drawn from the Universal Declaration of Human Rights.[1] These rights included:

153

rights to life and personal liberty, fair trial, freedom of speech and assembly, family rights, and the prohibition of torture. Certain provisions including the prohibition of torture were declared to be absolute, while other rights including freedom of speech and the right to a fair trial might be suspended 'at times of war or other public emergency' (art. 15).

The Convention provides two distinct procedures of enforcement: any state which is party to the Convention may complain before the European Commission of Human Rights about 'any alleged breach of the protections of the Convention' within the territory of another state (art. 24); an individual, where his state has accepted the right of individual petition, may directly petition the Commission concerning alleged violation of rights by his government (art. 25).

The inter-state procedure has not been frequently invoked. Political considerations must be weighed before one state will publicly accuse another of violating human rights. Only seven inter-state cases have been considered by the Commission since it was constituted.[2] It was this procedure which the government of the Irish Republic invoked in December 1971 against the British government, complaining of violation of rights and freedoms in Northern Ireland.

Under traditional international law an individual's rights could only be raised indirectly through the intervention of his own government. The principal innovation of the European Convention was to give the individual standing in his own right before an international tribunal. The British government is among the states which has accepted this optional article, and the resulting right of individual petition was relied on by a number of citizens in Northern Ireland between 1968 and 1974.

Though there are few procedural barriers to inter-state applications, any individual petitioning the European Commission must satisfy two conditions before his complaint will be admitted. He must show himself to be a 'victim' of the alleged violation of rights, and that he has exhausted all domestic remedies according to the generally recognised rules of international law (arts. 26, 27(3)). This decision on admissibility which precedes the investigation of the merits of any petition is one of the most critical in the Convention procedures. At the end of 1972, the Commission

154

had received 5960 petitions of which 108, or less than 2 per cent, were declared admissible.[3]

If an individual or inter-state application is found to be admissible, the Commission then proceeds to an investigation of the allegations. If no friendly settlement can be negotiated between the parties, the Commission refers its report on whether there has been a violation of the Convention to the Committee of Ministers of the Council of Europe, who render the final decision (arts. 28, 30–32). Before the consideration by the Committee of Ministers (which is primarily a political body), either the Commission itself or the state involved (but not an individual) may invoke the appellate jurisdiction of the European Court of Human Rights (arts. 32, 44, 47, 48). The Court has jurisdiction over the interpretation and application of the Convention and may also render limited advisory opinions at the request of the Committee of Ministers; its decisions are final (arts. 45, 52; protocol No. 2). Either the Court or, alternatively, the Committee of Ministers, has the power to direct a party to the Convention to take specific measures to redress any violations which may have been found (arts. 32, 50–54).

Northern Irish Applications

The first attempt to raise the Northern Ireland situation before the European Commission of Human Rights proved abortive. In 1968 petitions were filed on behalf of twelve individuals and the Northern Ireland Civil Rights Association. The applications alleged violations of almost every substantive article of the Convention, including the compatibility of the Special Powers Act with the Convention, discrimination in housing, gerrymandering and the banning of the civil rights march in Londonderry on 5 October 1968. Compensation for the alleged victims was also sought.

These proceedings, which became known as the 'Northern Irish Cases', failed to be admitted.[4] From the outset a protracted wrangle developed between the Commission and the American lawyer engaged by the applicants about legal aid fees. This ended with the Commission refusing to accept any further submissions from the lawyer or to conduct further correspondence with him. Despite attempts to continue with the cases, the question of new legal representation proved insoluble, and the Commission citing a 'clear lack of interest in pursuing the applications' struck all the cases off its list before formally considering the question of admissibility.[5] It is possible to argue that had this attempt to raise many of the initial grievances of the minority community succeeded, events in Northern Ireland might have taken a different direction. However even if the complainants had pressed their case with more vigour and been better represented, it is more likely that the protracted nature of investigations by the Commission would have nullified any direct influence of the cases on the developing crisis in Ulster.

There were numerous other applications to the European Commission of which two were of particular importance: the inter-state case brought by the Republic of Ireland against the United Kingdom,[6] and the applications of seven individuals, filed as *Donnelly and others v. The United Kingdom*.[7]

Following the revelations about interrogation in depth of persons detained for internment in August and September 1971, the government of the Republic of Ireland, acting in part under domestic political pressures, complained to the European Commission at Strasbourg in December 1971 about human rights violations in Northern Ireland by the British authorities. The Republic complained specifically about the compatability with the Convention of certain 'legislative measures', notably the Special Powers Act (arts. 5 and 6), and about 'administrative practices', notably the British government's failure to protect the right to life (art. 2), its sanctioning or permitting of brutality and torture during interrogation (art. 3), and the exercise of powers of detention without trial and the use of the security forces in a discriminatory manner (arts. 8 and 14). A second petition was filed on 3 March 1972, complaining of the retrospective nature of the Northern Ireland Act 1972 (art. 7). However, on an undertaking given by the United Kingdom government during the oral hearings on admissibility that no-one would be prosecuted under the Act for actions which were not crimes when

156

committed, the Irish government agreed to withdraw its second petition.[8]

It was not until September 1972 that oral hearings were held at Strasbourg on the admissibility of the complaints. In its decision of 1 October 1972 the Commission declared the application partially admissible; the complaint about discriminatory searches of Catholic homes by the security forces was abandoned by the Irish government, and the Commission declared inadmissible the allegation concerning violation of the right to life by the British security forces, because 'substantial evidence' had not been adduced to support it. The investigations of the merits of the application were opened in November 1973. These continued at intervals during 1974, and were expected to be completed by the spring of 1975.

The individual applications, *Donnelly and others v. the United Kingdom,* were subject to similar lengthy delays. The seven individuals involved complained in May 1972 of having been subjected to 'torture and inhuman or degrading treatment' contrary to Article 3 of the Convention, and sought to have their case treated as an emergency application. Despite being given precedence for their petition, the stage of investigation on the merits had not been completed by the end of 1974. Other individual applications filed after the inter-state case and the *Donnelly* case, which raised similar issues, either concerning detention without trial or torture, were left to await the outcome of these cases.

Enforcement of the Convention; Sanctions, Remedies and Impact

A question frequently raised by legal and lay commentators alike is whether, even when complaints are found to be justified, decisions by international tribunals like the European Commission and Court are effective. Though there is no international police force ready to enforce judgments directly, the legal and political obligations of the signatories to the Convention are clear. Parties to the Convention have undertaken a duty 'to secure to everyone within their jurisdiction the rights and freedoms' set forth in the Convention (art. 1), but they have further specifically agreed to abide by decisions of the Committee of Ministers and the Court of Human Rights (arts. 32(4), 53). With the exception of Greece, which denounced the Convention when it became certain that the Commission and the Committee of Ministers would find serious violations of the Convention, every other decision of the Commission, Committee of Ministers or Court has been complied with by the offending state, often as part of a friendly settlement encouraged by the Commission's procedures. Particularly within the context of growing economic and political integration in Europe, it can reasonably be expected that adherence to decisions taken under the Convention will continue to be the norm rather than the exception.

No specific sanctions are mentioned in the terms of the Convention itself; the Committee of Ministers may take 'measures' where a violation has been found and, if the offending state does not take satisfactory action, the Committee then decides 'what effect shall be given to its original decision and shall publish the Report' of the Commission (art. 32). Judgments of the Court must contain 'operative provisions' and be sent to the Committee of Ministers for execution (art. 54).

It is evident that the most important sanction envisaged by the Convention to secure execution of a judgment is the force of public opinion and international political pressure. While such indirect or moral pressures are limited in their effect, as is demonstrated only too clearly by the Greek case, international publicity remains a formidable weapon against many governments, particularly those responsible domestically to an electorate, and sensitive to the views of allies.

The only specific remedy mentioned in the Convention is that of compensation (art. 50), but it is clear that redress under the Convention is not limited to monetary awards. Other remedies that could be sought on an application to the Commission include: a permanent injunction against a certain course of conduct by the state concerned; a declaration that legislation is incompatible with the Convention, which would create an obligation on the part of the state to revoke it; a requirement that a state take affirmative action to uphold its obligations under the Convention, for instance, admission of an immigrant, release from prison of an applicant, discontinuance of criminal proceedings; and recommendations for procedural changes in domestic institutions to ensure that rights will not be violated in the future. It was relief of this nature rather than compensation that was sought in the Irish cases. Though no sanctions have yet been imposed on the United Kingdom and no remedies awarded to alleged victims, the proceedings at Strasbourg have probably had some effect on British policy. The limitation of the Northern Ireland Act 1972 was the most obvious result of appeal to the Commission.

More generally it is clear that after 1972 the United Kingdom government was conscious of its international obligations in its policy towards Northern Ireland. The proceedings in Strasbourg emphasised the anomalies of the situation prior to direct rule, when the Westminster government was internationally responsible for Northern Ireland but had little effective control over the internal affairs of the province. This point was clearly expressed in the 1972 Green Paper on Northern Ireland:

> For the future any arrangements must ensure that the United Kingdom Government has an effective and a determining voice in relation to any circumstances which involve, or may involve in the future, the commitment of the Armed Forces, the use of emergency powers, or repercussions at international level (para. 79).[9]

In particular the decision to repeal the Special Powers Act was certainly influenced by the complaints at Strasbourg against its provisions and discriminatory application, and the Northern Ireland (Emergency Provisions) Act 1973, passed by the Westminster Parliament, reflected the influence of the Convention in its drafting, particularly in the machinery of administrative detention.

The existence of the Convention and its requirements also played a part in the decision to abandon the techniques of interrogation investigated by the Compton Inquiry. It was largely because of the use of these techniques that the Irish government had complained at Strasbourg of an 'administrative practice' of torture. In the period following direct rule and particularly during 1973 the Strasbourg cases may also have had a bearing on decisions to prosecute a number of soldiers and policemen.

The efficacy of domestic remedies was an important issue in cases involving allegations against the security forces, and it is likely that the authorities were induced as a result to insist on a more thorough investigation and consideration of the possibility of prosecution, particularly in cases where torture was alleged. After the Strasbourg proceedings were instituted new and more detailed instructions were issued to the security forces concerning the treatment of persons while under arrest and interrogation, which emphasised the prohibition on brutality and warned that prosecutions could result from complaints.

On the other hand the impact of the Strasbourg cases must not be exaggerated.[10] The terms of the European Convention were relied on in the Northern Ireland (Emergency Provisions) Act 1973 to justify the admission in evidence of any confession which had not been obtained by torture or inhuman treatment, though the pre-existing common law rules were a good deal more restrictive. The requirement in the Convention that the cross-examination of witnesses was an indispensible part of a criminal trial was also used indirectly by the Diplock Committee as a justification for the maintenance of a system of administrative detention rather than the suspension of the right of cross-examination in specially constituted courts. More generally the long delays in the proceedings under the Convention ensured that when and if an adverse decision was reached, the British government could readily argue that the system had already been changed to avoid the recurrence of any abuses.

NOTES AND REFERENCES

1. On the Convention and its interpretation see R. Beddard *Human Rights and Europe* London 1973; J. E. S. Fawcett *The Application of the European Convention* Oxford 1969.
2. These cases were: two cases involving the Cyprus conflict in the 1950s (*Greece v. the United Kingdom* 2 Yearbook of the European Commission of Human Rights 182, 187); *Austria v. Italy* 4 Yearbook 116; the applications filed against Greece by four governments in 1967 (*Denmark et al. v. Greece* 12 bis Yearbook); and two applications arising out of the Northern Ireland situation (*Ireland v. United Kingdom* 41 Collected Decisions 3).
3. *Annual Report of European Commission on Human Rights* 1972, p. 35.

4. Application No. 3625 and others, 'Northern Irish Cases', 13 Yearbook 340–437.
5. 13 Yearbook 434.
6. Application No. 5310/71.
7. Application Nos. 5577/72 – 5583/72.
8. Application No. 5451/72; 41 Collected Decisions 3. See further chapter 7.
9. *The Future of Northern Ireland, a paper for discussion* 1972; see also *Northern Ireland Constitutional Proposals* Cmnd. 5259, London 1973, paras. 95, 114.
10. See generally 'Ireland in Strasbourg' by H. Hannum and K. Boyle, *The Irish Jurist* Vol. VII, p. 329.

9. THE HISTORICAL DIMENSION

Although certain features of the present situation in Northern
Ireland are unique, notably the scale of the conflict and the toll
of fatalities, there are other features which reflect patterns of
earlier social and political conflict, both within Ulster and in the
traditionally more disturbed provinces of Southern Ireland, over
the past two hundred years. This chapter is intended to set the
contemporary troubles in a more general historical perspective,
illustrating some of the continuities in both conflict and response.

The Eighteen Century and the Protestant Ascendancy

The emergence of settled administration in Ireland dates from
the second half of the eighteenth century. In 1769 the English
government appointed a permanent government in Dublin,
headed by a resident Viceroy, the Lord Lieutenant for Ireland.
For the previous five centuries, from the time of the arrival of
the first English armies whose soldiers comprised the initial
settlers, the country, when not in contest between native Irish
and the English, had been administered on an ad hoc basis, by
irregularly constituted local parliaments and caretaker function-
aries, known as Lord Justices, appointed from the colonist
gentry.

The relatively stable conditions of the mid-eighteenth century
derived from the effect on Ireland of the revolutionary wars and
constitutional settlement of 1689–91. The Protestant colony in
Ireland had emerged victorious from the contest between
William of Orange and James II for the English throne. The

native population, which had rallied to the cause of James, thereby finally lost all prospect of driving out the English army or the settlers.

The Anglican gentry who were now in complete control proceeded to entrench their position by the notorious system of laws known as the Penal Code. This code, in accord with the prevailing religious intolerance of the times, was directed against the Ulster colonists, who were predominantly dissenters, and the native Roman Catholics alike. Their chief intent was to neutralise the threat of Roman Catholic numbers by preventing them from obtaining economic and political power. Roman Catholics were prohibited from holding land other than on short leases, they were denied access to education and excluded from all administrative, judicial or political office. These restrictions also applied, though less systematically, to the Northern Presbyterians. In this way the tiny Anglican landed minority, which never constituted more than one-tenth of the population, achieved a monopoly of political authority.

The extent to which the numerous and frequently pettifogging provisions of the Penal Code were ever enforced awaits detailed study. Certainly from the mid-eighteenth century onwards, the code was gradually relaxed and by the end of the century it had almost entirely collapsed in the backwash of both the American and French Revolutions. But this century of complete Protestant ascendancy decisively shaped the character of Irish society for the future. The relationship which it cemented of superordination and subordination between settler and native, with its components of religious, national and class differences, had a pervasive influence on the evolving political and legal systems of the country.

One consequence of particular significance for the nineteenth century was an alienation on the part of Roman Catholics from the law, which may be traced to the peasantry's experience of Protestant justice in the seventeenth and eighteenth centuries.[1] This alienation was in all probability culturally transmitted, but it was continually reinforced throughout the eighteenth and nineteenth centuries by new experience of coercion and force at the hands both of the local Irish government and of its British masters.

The second half of the eighteenth century also saw the beginnings of the complex pattern of agrarian disturbance and political agitation which was to be such a distinctive feature of Irish history for the next hundred years.

In 1761 in the impoverished province of Munster there were sporadic attacks on the property of local landlords and the Anglican clergy. These incidents were prompted by the heavy burdens on the peasantry of rent and tythe and were claimed by groups of peasants variously styled as 'Levellers' or 'Whiteboys'. Open meetings were held and threatening notices posted on the gables of churches and estates. In a few areas recently enclosed commons were reclaimed for common use and landlords' cattle were houghed. The Whiteboys proclaimed what they thought to be a fair rent and tythe and ordered the peasantry to pay no more. These 'primitive rebels' were neither well-organised nor particularly violent. The disturbances were localised and thus easily suppressed, and were put down with great cruelty. But a similar form of agrarian unrest emerged again in the 1780s. This time the peasants were better organised in clandestine oath-bound societies which proved more difficult to contain or suppress.[2]

These disturbances were the forerunners of an enduring pattern of agrarian conflict and coercive response which continued in cycles throughout the nineteenth century. Their special significance was to make clear the ineffectiveness of the existing system of local administration, and to pave the way for the introduction of a totally new system of government in Ireland.

In theory the structure of local administration in eighteenth century Ireland was identical to that of England. The system was based on the assumption that local property owners should police their own areas. From the parish unit up to the county grand jury everything was dependent on the exertions of the local gentry and more prosperous tenantry. Responsibility for virtually all aspects of local administration and for the maintenance of law and order, including the raising of the necessary finance, rested on them. This feudal system of social control was already under strain in England as the process of urbanisation gathered pace. In Ireland, where the population was still almost wholly rural, it should have lasted longer, but in practice it probably never functioned effectively.

The obvious reason for this was the division of the population into hostile ethnic groups. Since the political system excluded the Roman Catholic majority from any form of participation, the whole burden of local administration fell on the small Protestant minority. Except in Ulster the Protestant population was thinly spread, and especially so in the poorer regions of the South and West where the disturbances were concentrated. A further problem was absenteeism. Many of the landed proprietors from whose numbers the magistracy might have been drawn lived in England, and regarded their estates in Ireland merely as a source of income. Those who were resident in Ireland and played their part in local administration appear from the evidence available to have been corrupt, inefficient and partisan, especially in their capacity as Justices of the Peace. The openly Protestant character of the magistracy further exacerbated the difficulties of maintaining law and order and reinforced the bonds of sympathy between the peasants and the secret societies.

The natural result of this situation was that responsibility for maintaining order rested largely on the central government and on the British army. Throughout the eighteenth century, despite great constitutional hostility to a standing army, large numbers of soldiers were engaged more or less continuously in internal policing in Ireland. The practice of dispersing the regular army throughout the country in small units was a constant complaint of military commanders throughout the eighteenth and early-nineteenth centuries. In 1787 the Commander-in-Chief wrote as follows:

> The King's troops have been fully employed in assisting to collect the revenue, and to carry into execution the common and statute law, in supporting the King's writs and suppressing tumultous risings . . . nor do I hesitate to add that but for the military there would be no government at all.[3]

As the years passed the army became increasingly indispensible to the conduct of government and it was eventually agreed that the office of Lord Lieutenant, or chief civilian executive, should be held by a military chief. In 1797 one official commented, in support of this proposal, that 'the government had now become so intermixed with military measures, which military measures were so connected with the politics of the country, that the Lord Lieutenant ought to be a military man'.[4]

But then as now there was a limit to what could be achieved by military force. For the system of prosecutions under the criminal law to function effectively it was essential to have information and evidence on the identity of offenders. The only source of this in most cases was the peasantry. But as long as the law was represented by Protestant landlords or clergymen, whose financial exactions were their chief grievance, little co-operation could be expected from the Catholic peasantry. This reluctance to give information was reinforced by the knowledge that the rural guerrillas meted out certain and severe punishment to anyone assisting in the prosecution of a Whiteboy.

The response of the government to the continuing disturbances was to concentrate soldiers in large numbers in the disaffected areas in the hope of overawing the peasantry and deterring the peasant associations. In addition the magistrates and troops were granted extraordinary summary powers in a series of statutes passed in the Irish parliament, known as the Whiteboy Acts. These authorised the imposition of curfews, and the arrest, search, compulsory interrogation and summary trial of suspects, and prohibited all assemblies of peasantry. A wide range of new capital offences was created including the taking or giving of oaths.

Despite these draconian powers and widespread deployment of troops peasant disaffection spread in the closing years of the century. In the 1780s there were outbreaks of disorder in Ulster centred on the activities of local associations of tenants, known as Oakboys, in protest against taxes and evictions, in addition to continuing unrest in Munster. These disorders in Ulster developed in the 1790s into a sectarian conflict between Roman Catholic and Protestant tenants out of which grew the Orange Order. In an increasingly violent situation the Orange movement spread throughout the country and was matched by a new, more political Roman Catholic organisation, the Defenders. In 1797–98 the Roman Catholics rose in armed rebellion under the leadership of a group of Northern Presbyterian radicals. The English government inevitably sided with the loyal Protestants who were organised and armed in local forces of yeomanry. Powers of internment were used for the first time to detain the leaders of the rebellion, which was eventually put down with great bloodshed.[5] The local hatred between Roman Catholic and Protestant which was aroused in those years was to survive for a considerable period after the conflict. The abortive rebellion also hastened the radical restructuring of legal administration undertaken in the following century.

The Professionalisation of Justice in the Nineteenth Century

The Act of Union 1800, which joined Ireland to England in an 'indissoluble' union and abolished the separate Irish parliament and administration, was accepted by influential Roman Catholics in return for a promise that full civil rights for all citizens and the impartial administration of law and order would be guaranteed. In the early years of the new century the English government faced continuing political pressure on this commitment, in addition to the persistent problem of agrarian violence and the pressing need to find some substitute for the regular army in the countryside.[6]

The solution which gradually evolved was the professionalisation of justice. In the place of the existing piecemeal system for the maintenance of rural order a new form of rational and bureaucratic machinery for legal administration was constructed, specifically designed to cope with the sectarian and ethnic divisions and the recurrent turbulence of the Irish countryside. This new system of administration set a pattern for later changes in England itself, and provided a lasting prototype for future British colonial legal administration.

The first important step was the assertion of state control over criminal prosecutions in the courts. Formerly it had been left to individual citizens to take the initiative, and this had been one of the chief weaknesses in the enforcement system, particularly in

167

the rural areas where the pressures on the individual victims of crime not to prosecute or testify were great. From 1801 Crown Solicitors were appointed to each court circuit whose duty it was to conduct prosecutions at assizes, particularly of agrarian and political crimes, under the direction of the Attorney-General. The central government bore the expense of prosecution including the costs of witnesses. This system survived in Northern Ireland until the creation of the office of Director of Public Prosecutions in 1972, which was designed to ensure a clear separation between the government and those responsible for law enforcement. In the nineteenth century no such separation was mooted; the responsibility for instituting prosecutions was directly and openly linked to the government of the day and no-one conceived that it should be otherwise.[7]

The second step was the creation of a permanent police force. In 1820 Robert Peel, then Chief Secretary for Ireland, reorganised the temporary and emergency police establishments then in existence into a centralised County Constabulary. This new force was organised on military lines, like a continental gendarmerie. It was armed, mounted and quartered in barracks throughout the country. But its duties extended not only to maintaining order and arresting suspects, but also to prosecuting in the petty courts. The new police constabulary was from the start directly responsible to the central authorities and ultimately the local share of the cost of the force was taken over by the central Exchequer.

The final step was the replacement of the local Justices of the Peace, the voluntary magistracy, by a system of legally trained stipendiaries under government control. The new magistrates became known as Resident Magistrates from the requirement that they should reside in the 'station' assigned to them. They combined both executive and judicial roles: the constabulary was under their direction at the local level, in particular in dealing with disturbances or riots; and they presided as justices in the local courts, which from 1827 were reorganised in a new system of regular petty sessions. In addition the existing lists of voluntary magistrates were purged and for the first time a number of Roman Catholics were appointed.

The effect of this pattern of intervention in the traditional structures of local government was gradually to 'de-Protestantise' the administration of justice at the local level. Though for a considerable period most of the President Magistrates were still Protestants, they were generally outsiders and to that extent impartial in local conflicts, unlike the landlords of the voluntary magistracy that they replaced whose partiality was notorious. The new constabulary, the majority of which was Roman Catholic, was also less obviously partisan, and the authorities were at pains to exclude both Orange and Roman Catholic militants from joining.

Public attitudes to the judicial system also began to change. Though Daniel O'Connell, for a long period the political leader of the Roman Catholic masses and himself a lawyer, did not finally win emancipation for the Roman Catholics until 1829, he had few complaints to make about discrimination in the courts when he was questioned on the subject by a House of Lords committee in 1825. He did complain of the activities of Orange juries and the Orange yeomanry in the North, but he declared that generally the judiciary at all levels was unbiased in its dealings with Roman Catholics. But religious consciousness about law remained, as shown by O'Connell's reply to a question on the new professional magistracy:

Q. Do you think the Catholics [of Munster] have any reason to complain of the conduct of the magistrates in point of partiality in the administration of justice?

A. The system has left just this impression upon their minds that in all cases when they are before the magistrates it would be better for them to be Protestants than Catholics.[8]

This kind of thinking about the legal system was deeply engrained in both communities and was never entirely to disappear. Nevertheless the policy of professionalisation was pursued with some success. Though the whole legal system remained distinctly Protestant in the North, offices at all levels of the central judicial administration and the civil service were gradually opened to Roman Catholics. Lord O'Hagan, first Catholic Lord Chancellor, and also the first Catholic judge, was appointed in 1968.[9]

The effect of the centralisation and professionalisation of justice in producing a degree of confidence in and support for government was most marked among middle-class urban Catholics. The position was radically different in the rural counties, where the bulk of the population lived and where the coercive authority of the state was most apparent. There was little prospect of the new administration gaining the support of the peasantry as long as the courts and the police continued to enforce the same unjust laws.

The principal and continuing grievance of the peasantry was the tythe. But as the century progressed there developed a more general campaign for tenants rights. In one form or another the dominant issue of the nineteenth century in Ireland was land, and the respective rights of tiller and landlord in relation to it. The complex story of the ensuing struggle for land reform cannot be dealt with here,[10] but certain general features of the situation were significant.

In the first place the pattern of the disturbances which broke out from time to time was similar to that of the previous century. Most were centred on grievances which were essentially local in effect. The peasants who took part formed themselves into oath-bound secret societies which terrorised landlords and tythe collectors and burned their property. Informers and others who defied the societies were liable to be attacked and maimed. On a number of occasions throughout the century, however, simple peasant violence was converted into mass civil disobedience under the leadership of a succession of national political figures. During these campaigns local disturbances almost completely ceased, but would soon break out again when the politicians apparently failed to achieve any immediate reforms. The outstanding examples of this pattern were Daniel O'Connell's campaigns for emancipation and tythe abolition, and the Land League Campaign of the 1880s led by Charles Stewart Parnell.

The response of the English government to both types of campaign was an infinite variation of the policy of coercion and conciliation, or 'kicks and kindness' as it became derisively known. This approach was perhaps inevitable given the delicate and complex relationships between English politics, the landlord class and the peasantry. The motives for complaint about agrarian 'outrage' on the part of the Irish landlords were certainly as political as the motives of the peasants for indulging in violence. Most of the numerous parliamentary inquiries into crime in Ireland in the nineteenth century were initiated by loyalist and landlord interests, and designed to produce evidence to beat the government with. On the other hand the government was at times sincere in its search for what it conceived to be a just and peaceful solution.

The resulting political struggle between the government and the landlords may help to explain why the scale of rural disorder was much exaggerated. Despite the outbreaks of rural terrorism the crime rate in Ireland appears to have been generally remarkably low throughout the century, even for a country so little urbanised as Ireland. The vast majority of offences even in the most violent years in the second half of the century were urban rather than rural, and comprised in the main undramatic offences of larceny for gain and drunkenness. The most characteristic and prevalent form of agrarian crime complained of and recorded throughout the century was 'intimidation'. Though real threats were clearly made and occasionally carried out, the phenomenon of intimidation reflected in essence a contest of will between the peasantry and the landlords with the latter insisting and relying on government force. The most violent incidents usually arose out of such set-piece confrontations as evictions or the enforced sale of cattle seized to pay for rents. In these the peasantry usually fared badly against the soldiers or constabulary.

To this extent the landlord interest always appeared to prevail. Whatever the merits of the peasantry's demands (and most were eventually conceded) the immediate and simplest remedy of coercion was always the first official resort. The sheer bulk of the repressive laws, or Coercion Acts, passed for Ireland in the nineteenth century is impressive. Peel noted in 1829 that 'for scarcely a year during the period that has elapsed since the Union has Ireland been governed by the ordinary course of law'.[11] It may be added that from the date of Peel's comment to the end of the Union in 1920 there were equally few years when the ordinary rule of law applied. In the period from 1800 to 1900 at least seventy-three separate statutes of a coercive character were passed for Ireland. Detention without trial (suspension of *habeas corpus*) was introduced on four different occasions for a total of eleven years.

A further indication of the nature of the conflict is the fact that, despite the introduction of the new police force, it was well into the century before the regular army was removed from the front line in disturbed areas. Again in 1829, Peel remarked with some exasperation that 'in the course of the last six months, England being at peace with the whole world has had five-sixths of the infantry force of the United Kingdom occupied in maintaining the peace and in police duties in Ireland'.[12] As the numbers of men in the constabulary increased, army strength in Ireland declined. But until the middle of the century, while the population of Ireland was roughly half that of England and Wales, the number of soldiers stationed in Ireland was rarely less than and at times exceeded the number in Britain, as shown in Table 9.1. In the latter part of the century British colonial policy led to the withdrawal of troops to home barracks in Britain, but the garrison in Ireland remained remarkably high for a country with a rapidly declining population.

TABLE 9.1:   *The number of British troops in Ireland, Great Britain and Scotland for selected years, 1792 – 1923*

Year	Ireland		Great Britain		Scotland	
	Total	No. per 100,000	Total	No. per 100,000	Total	No. per 100,000
1792	11,113	235†	15,764	180†		
1822	22,381	324	18,621	128	2,321	109
1830	23,621	308	23,178	160		
1842	17,771	216	21,288	113		
1861	25,025	432	72,760	314	4,307	140
1872	27,211	506	73,474	277	3,469	102
1883	24,614	490	62,121	204	3,336	88
1906	25,006	569	100,148	257	5,585	121
1911	26,438	603	101,322	248	4,806	101
1921	57,116	1,312	73,412	171	5,030	103
1923	4,399*	349	87,692	202	4,546	93

* Northern Ireland only
† Approximate figure

Police strength was also considerable. By 1864 there were 13,800 in the constabulary for a population which had been depleted from eight million to less than six million by the Great Famine of the 1840s. This compared with a total in England and Wales of 23,600 for a population almost four times as great. The overall ratio of police to citizen in Ireland in 1863, calculated on a county basis, was 1 in 417 with a maximum of 1 in 195 in the most troubled districts. For England and Wales the average was 1 in 887, with a maximum of 1 in 417.[13] The figures in Table 9.2 for police strength per 100,000 in Ireland, England and Wales, and Scotland for selected years throughout the century give a very clear indication of the extent to which Ireland was both earlier and more heavily policed than other parts of the United Kingdom.

TABLE 9.2: *Police strength in Ireland, England & Wales and Scotland for selected years, 1835–1897*

Year	Ireland		England & Wales		Scotland	
	Total	No. per 100,000	Total	No. per 100,000	Total	No. per 100,000
1835–36	8,423	106	4,751	32	614	24
1838–39	9,217	114	6,101	40	684	27
1842–43	10,399	126	10,567	66	1,091	41
1847–48	12,188	152	11,876	69	1,146	41
1851–52	13,565	208	13,232	74	1,824	63
1867	13,302	242	24,073*	111	2,804	86
1877	12,456	236	30,016	122	3,241	90
1887	13,977	288	36,912	133	3,892	99
1897	12,900	285	42,140	135	4,707	109

* After the County Constabulary Act 1857

These efforts at legal repression were undoubtedly effective for a time. The suspension of *habeas corpus* and the arrest of militant leaders probably frustrated serious attempts at revolution on at least three occasions: in 1803, in 1848 and in 1866–67. The weight of police numbers and the efficient administration of summary justice maintained order in the rural areas at most times. The system of coercion also bought time for the varied attempts at legislative reform of the land problem, which eventually arrived at the solution of peasant proprietorship.

Yet the costs of repression were high in terms of the

173

cumulative alienation of the bulk of the population from the government and the state. The underlying hostility of the peasantry to the law and its administration gave considerable impetus to the spread of nationalist feeling among the rural population. The new machinery of bureaucratised justice had been relatively successful in healing the local divisions between Roman Catholic and Protestant, but it could not hope to win acceptance for the state when the conflict took on a new dimension with the emergence of an Irish nationalist consciousness. The growth of Irish Nationalism and its counterpart of Unionism in Ulster in the late-nineteenth century could only emphasise the *political* element in law and its administration. The reforms which had earlier been designed to free the administration of justice from all suspicion of sectarian bias or partisanship served now to increase its isolation. The centralised judicial system, the professional magistracy, the police, were all perceived as instruments of executive justice, and of an English executive at that. Once trust was lost in the British government of Ireland as a whole, the local instruments of central control also became suspect. Wherever the system of justice depended on the local population for its effective operation, it failed. It became particularly evident in the new phase of nationalist feeling that the state had lost control of the jury room in criminal trials.

The Jury Problem

The continued existence of the jury at all in Ireland in this period is remarkable. Repressive policies would have been a good deal easier to execute if the trial of serious crime had involved only the professional judiciary. But it was part of the complexity of English rule in Ireland that its repressive policies were pursued through law, and were to a considerable degree bound by the same corpus of common law institutions and values that had grown up in England over the centuries. There were frequent departures in principle and practice from those legal traditions, as has been explained, but for most of the nineteenth century that most hallowed right of English law, trial by common jury, was preserved even in Ireland.

But trial by jury did not function in Ireland as it did in England. Irish juries would not convict, either at all on some occasions, or to an extent that would satisfy the regime that the guilty were being dealt with. The reasons were obvious. The jurymen felt closer to the prisoner than the prosecutor, and where the offence charged had a political or an agrarian flavour the prevailing community pressure was usually strong enough to ensure that even an independent minded juror brought home a not guilty verdict. Throughout the century an extraordinary amount of thought and effort was expended by successive administrations in an attempt to resolve the contradiction of using popular tribunals to enforce unpopular laws. Prosecutors and prisoners alike devoted their energy to the task of getting the 'best' jury for their respective purposes. 'Packing' juries was a notorious but accepted procedure by both government and people. Early in the century the regime had the advantage since the jury list was restricted to property owners, most of whom were Protestants. By intelligent use of the right to challenge jurors, convictions could be reasonably assured, though at the price of renewed accusations of religious discrimination and bias. The most famous packed jury was that which convicted Daniel O'Connell himself in 1844, a conviction ultimately quashed by the House of Lords on the ground that such practices make trial by jury 'a delusion, a mockery and a snare'.[14]

In the last quarter of the century the rapidly increasing nationalist feeling and a new burst of land agitation coincided with a broadening of the jury franchise. As a result the government at times virtually lost control of law enforcement for indictable crime. At times during the 1870s acquittals at the rural assizes were returned in as many as 75 per cent of the cases tried. Assizes were sometimes even abandoned when it became evident that no proper trials were possible. In 1881 a House of Lords inquiry into the Irish jury problem recommended the obvious solution, the suspension of trial by jury for political or agrarian crime.[15] Legislation was duly enacted in 1882 to provide for non-jury trial. But the outcry both from the powerful Irish parliamentary party and from the Irish judiciary ensured that the new powers were never used. Instead coercion limped on with the use of 'special juries' of property owners and an extension of the powers of summary trial, until unrest and violence melted away when the land problem was finally solved in the 1890s by buying out the landlords. There followed a few peaceful years before the renewal of the political struggle in 1912.

The Northern Dimension

For most of the nineteenth century the history of the North of Ireland can be recounted separately from that of the South. The region around Belfast shared in the industrial revolution and prosperity of England and Scotland. As a result the bonds of nationality, race and culture between Protestant Ulster and the rest of Britain were maintained and strengthened, and the degree of identification with Dublin and the rural South of Ireland progressively declined. The contrast between North and South was also heightened by the relative prosperity and security of the Ulster tenant farmer who knew nothing of the deprivation or the struggles of the Southern peasantry.

As a result the North tended to be unaffected by the upheavals of the century in the rest of Ireland. There was much less rural violence, conflict was political rather than social or economic in nature, and centred as today on the relations between a Protestant majority and a Roman Catholic minority. These communal attitudes naturally gave rise to complaints about partiality of justice. The source of most complaints about the administration of law was the influence of the ubiquitous Orange movement, which after the Union had gained a remarkable power among the Protestants. A parliamentary inquiry in 1835 heard evidence that its influence was considerable in the army, magistracy and the administration of local justice generally.[16] A chief complaint was that juries in the rural counties were frequently packed with Orangemen and that neither in civil nor criminal cases could Roman Catholics expect justice from them. The Roman Catholics also complained about the sectarian activities of the local yeomanry, before they were disbanded in 1834.

The English government did make some attempt to remedy this problem by suppressing the Orange Order and banning provocative Orange marches under a series of Party Processions Acts in the 1840s. But these laws proved as ineffective as had similar legislation in suppressing the Catholic Association in the South. Violent confrontation between the Orange movement and the Roman Catholic ribbon societies in the rural areas continued throughout the century, though the incidents were relatively infrequent and of short duration. The most serious clashes occurred in urban settings, particularly in Belfast in the second half of the century. The main feature of these disturbances was repeated communal strife between the poorer Roman Catholics and Protestants in a few contiguous areas in the inner city. Economic fears on the part of the Protestants about the increasing Roman Catholic population coming in from rural areas may have been an element in the conflict, but the principal cause of sectarian violence was probably the political and religious hatred of the Roman Catholics which had been fanned by Protestant demagogues.[17]

The Dublin administration took advantage of the disturbances in 1860 to disband the local town police in Belfast, which an inquiry had shown to be both partisan and ineffective, and to bring what had by then become the Royal Irish Constabulary into the city. But in general terms the dominance of the Protestant power structure in the Northern counties remained unaffected. The centrally controlled system of Resident Magistrates made less impact in the North where the local gentry were industrious and for the most part permanently resident, and thus a good deal more effective as magistrates than their counterparts in the South. It was not until after the establishment of the new Unionist state in 1921 that the effect of the system of centralised and professional justice, based on state-appointed magistrates and a state-controlled police force, was fully felt in Northern Ireland. And by that time it was a firmly entrenched Protestant state which they represented and protected. At the risk of some oversimplification it might be claimed that the effect of the new centralised and bureaucratic system for the administration of justice combined with the progressive extension of the franchise under British legislation led in the southern part of Ireland to a new independent state and in Northern Ireland to an unstable sectarian state.[18]

NOTES AND REFERENCES

1. See, for example, *A History of Ireland in the Eighteenth Century* by W. B. H. Lecky, 1913, vol. 1, p. 272.
2. See generally *Secret Societies in Ireland* edited by T. D. Williams, 1973.
3. Quoted in *Irish Public Opinion 1750–1800* by R. B. M. McDowell, 1944, p. 50.
4. Quoted in *Great Britain and Ireland, 1760–1800: a study in political administration* by E.M. Johnston, 1963, p. 56.
5. *The Green Flag: A History of Irish Nationalism* by R. Kee, 1972, pp. 41–132.
6. *Rural Disorder and Police Reform in Ireland 1812–36* by G. Broeker, 1970, pp. 41–132.
7. See generally, *Report of Working Party on Public Prosecutions* Cmd. 554, Belfast 1971, Appendix A(1).
8. *Select Committee of the House of Lords on the State of Ireland* Evidence, P.P. 1825 *IX*, p. 133.
9. See generally, *The Irish Administration 1801–1914* by R. B. M. McDowell, 1964.
10. See *Ireland Since the Famine* by F. S. L. Lyons, revised ed. 1973, and references.
11. Quoted in *Coercive Measures in Ireland 1830–1880* by I. S. Leadam, Pamphlet National Press Agency, London 1881, p. 1.
12. Quoted in *Dublin Castle and the Irish People* by B. R. O'Brien, 1909, p. 60.
13. *Judicial Statistics for Ireland, 1863* P.P. 1864 *LVII*, pp. 653–71.
14. *O'Connell v. Regina* 8 E.R. 1061 (1841), per Lord Denman, at p. 1135.
15. *Report from the Select Committee of the House of Lords on Irish Jury Laws* 12 August 1881.
16. *Select Committee on Orange Lodges in Ireland,* P.P. 1835 *XVII*; and see H. Senior, *Orangeism in Ireland and Britain, 1795–1836* Routledge and Kegan Paul, 1966.
17. *Belfast: Approach to Crisis, A Study of Belfast Politics 1613–1970* by I. Budge and C. O'Leary, 1973, pp. 73–100; *Holy War in Belfast* by A. Boyd, 1969.
18. For the governmental and political history of Northern Ireland since 1920, see *Governing Without Consensus; An Irish Perspective* by Richard Rose, 1971.

10. CONCLUSION

The theme of this book has been that a legal system cannot be regarded as operating in a political vacuum. Yet the nature of the relationship between a state and its legal system is likely to vary in changing circumstances. In the case of Northern Ireland this relationship has been particularly complex, due to the differing demands and expectations of two major communal groupings within the state. Nonetheless some understanding of the situation can be gained by starting from the 'normal' state of affairs which may be expected to prevail in most unitary states, and working through a 'colonial' model towards a generalised account of the operation of a legal system in a deeply divided community.

In most states the legal system is likely to reflect the prevailing values and power structures, and to be generally accepted as so doing. In some cases the accepted value system may be class based, in the sense that the rights and duties of different social and economic classes will differ widely. In such conditions the legal system may be expected to provide an institutional structure for the support and maintenance of that class system. In others the value system on which the legal system is based may proclaim a greater measure of equality in the rights and duties of all citizens, without going very far to secure the equal enjoyment of those rights and duties. In a few the legal system may have played and continue to play an important part in maintaining a measure of social and economic equality. In all cases however the main focus of the legal system is likely to change when the existing state is threatened either by external attack or internal subversion. In these new and usually temporary circumstances the legal system is likely to be openly used by those in power

179

to suppress internal opposition, more or less regardless of the values which the legal system is thought to embody in more stable times. Again in so doing it is likely to have the support or at least the acquiescence of the bulk of the population. In times of emergency few will object if civil rights are denied to marginal members of society.

In a colonial situation, where there is unlikely to be the same degree of shared values and objectives between the settlers or conquerors and the native population, the oppressive and coercive nature of the legal system will be correspondingly more obvious and more permanent. There is no reason why oppression, when backed with sufficient military and economic power, should not prove effective over long periods. It may also in certain circumstances lead to a gradual acceptance by the settling and native population alike of a new set of shared values and objectives and thus to a new stability. But the continued use of the legal system to coerce and subdue the native population or to maintain the social and economic privileges of the settlers is equally likely to lead to an increasing alienation on the part of the native population from the law and state which it supports. In such cases, as in Southern Ireland in the eighteenth and nineteenth centuries, the government may be faced with the difficult choice of continuing with a policy of open coercion or of meeting the demands of the native population either for social or economic change, or else for political independence. Where the colonial government lacks either the power or the will to maintain itself by force in the face of such demands, a revolutionary settlement is the most likely outcome. This is particularly likely where the government is committed to such general principles as universal adult suffrage and equality before the law, and where the native population is so large as to make continued coercion either impractical or uneconomic.

In Northern Ireland this simple colonial model cannot be directly applied. The 'settlers' constitute two-thirds of the population and have always had sufficient economic and military force at their disposal to make continued coercion a practical proposition, more or less regardless of the extent of the alienation of the bulk of the 'native' minority from the legal system and the state. But the minority in Northern Ireland is large enough to ensure a continuing degree of instability within the state, and to render continuing coercion both politically embarrassing and economically damaging to the government and the people alike. In these circumstances it would be rational for a government to seek to use the legal system primarily as a means to greater co-operation rather than as an instrument of coercion, or at the least to use instruments of coercion with the utmost restraint and with maximum safeguards. Persistence in a policy of general coercion of the minority is likely to ensure that a state of instability will continue.

Within this broad framework it is also important to take account of the nature of the institutions of enforcement. Coercion, and conciliation, may be entrusted to a wide range of enforcement bodies. The legal system, the police, the Army and a paramilitary communal force, like the 'B Specials' in Northern Ireland, will each typically implement a given security policy and interpret a given legislative framework in a totally different way. The outcome of any internal emergency will thus depend on a large number of factors: the way in which the authorities perceive the problem, the legal and administrative framework on which they rely to deal with it, the internal structures and loyalties of the enforcement institutions, and the reaction of the population to them. In Northern Ireland, where there are two communal populations, and where the authorities have sought to operate both a military security and a civilian policing policy at the same time as a programme of political conciliation, it is scarcely surprising that the situation has become one of great complexity. But if there is any lesson to be learned from the five years of conflict from 1969 to 1974 it is that the choice of a security response to a crisis of intercommunal relations is likely to impede the restoration of stability.

Appendix A

METHODOLOGY AND STATISTICS

The purpose of this brief appendix is first to clarify the different statistical bases of the two sets of tables taken from our own and the Attorney-General's studies of the pre-Diplock trials in the first half of 1973, published in *Justice in Northern Ireland* and *Prosecutions in Northern Ireland* respectively; secondly to attempt to account for the apparent divergence in the conclusions drawn from these two studies; and thirdly to explain the rather different procedure adopted in our study of the Diplock trials.

Our own study of the Belfast City Commission cases was based on an analysis of all cases *set down for trial* in the relevant period, and thus included a number of cases which were subsequently adjourned to the Belfast Recorder's Court and a few in which the defendants failed to answer their bail. The Attorney-General's survey covered only those cases which were *actually tried* in the period from January to June. This difference accounts for the major discrepancies in the two sets of figures, and in particular those in respect of the total number of counts preferred against the various classes of defendants. Some other small discrepancies arose out of the difficulty in identifying the religion of some of the defendants – our own reworking of the material has revealed one case which it now appears was wrongly classified – and from the fact that our analysis included a number of counts which were put down for trial but never formally preferred and thus omitted from the Attorney-General's analysis. These differences clearly resulted in different totals being arrived at in the various analyses, but do not in our opinion affect the general validity of either of the two surveys. We have not attempted for that reason to produce a detailed comparative analysis of the two surveys, which would probably serve only to confuse the ordinary reader still further.

For the purposes of this book the main divergence arises between Table 6.2, taken from the Attorney-General's analysis, and Table 6.3, taken from our own study. In the first place the analysis in Table 6.2 is based on the combinations of charges preferred against each individual defendant, which we accept as the best indication of the point at issue, namely the tendency to omit the least serious 'no certificate' charges in cases involving Roman Catholics. A reworking of our own figures, which include the batch of adjourned cases already referred to, produced a broadly similar pattern to that shown in Table 6.2. The further analysis in Table 6.3, however, does help to clarify the type of case in which the difference in approach appears to have been greatest, despite the different method of analysis based on the total number of charges preferred against all defendants in each category. The Attorney-General's attempt to duplicate this table appears to have used different criteria for distinguishing the circumstances of the searches, and hence produced a somewhat different result. A further analysis of our own material has confirmed our suspicion that some of the apparent discrimination was founded in the difference in approach between persons found with handguns and rifles, which is discussed in greater detail in respect of the Diplock trials (see pages 105–116). There was nonetheless a clear difference in the overall approach to cases in which Protestants and Roman Catholics respectively were found in the street or in cars with handguns, if cases of robbery and actual shooting are excluded: a new analysis of our material on the basis of the combination of charges against each individual has revealed that 'no certificate' charges were included against 30 out of 41 Protestants found with handguns compared with only 10 out of 27 Roman Catholics. It should be noted that there was one single case in which 16 individual Protestants were found together with a number of pistols and shotguns and all charged with 'no certificate' offences; even if these are omitted there was still a substantial difference with 'no certificate' charges being included against 14 out of 25 Protestants compared with 10 out of 27 Roman Catholics.

In a more general context it may also be noted that the

Attorney-General's study in seeking to isolate the performance of the prosecuting officers under his control appears to us to have missed at least some of the point of our criticisms, which was that there was a cumulative difference in treatment resulting from small differences in approach at various stages in the trial process. The prosecuting authorities were able to produce adequate reasons for each individual decision on the withdrawal of charges, as shown in the appendix to their study, but we are not satisfied that in so doing they gave sufficient attention to the overall impact of the resulting pattern on public confidence, or that they took as much care as some at least of the judges to counteract the danger of biased findings by juries. When we published our findings we were equally aware of the fact that they would be given wide publicity and that in the interests of easy presentation on radio and television and in the press an over-simplified picture would be given of our position. We deliberately took this risk in the hope that the authorities could thus be induced to take more seriously the need to convince the minority community of the absolute equality of treatment of all defendants. We believe that despite the apparent conflict between our own and the Attorney-General's conclusion our work has had some beneficial effect in this context.

Finally it should be noted that in preparing our analysis of the results of the Diplock trials we have adopted a different form of analysis, based on a consideration of the combination of charges and outcomes in each separate trial, regardless of the number of defendants and charges. For this purpose the most serious charges, convictions and sentences were used. This difference in approach was based on the experience of our own and the Attorney-General's analysis of the pre-Diplock material, and though it means that the studies of the pre-Diplock and post-Diplock cases are not strictly comparable, we are satisfied that it gives a better picture of the trial process as a whole.

CASES

INDEX

193